ROBERT H. MCNEAL, editor of this volume, is Associate Professor of History and a member of the Centre for Russian and East European Studies at the University of Toronto. He is the author of *The Bolshevik Tradition: Lenin, Stalin, Khrushchev,* and the editor of *Lenin, Stalin, Khrushchev: Voices of Bolshevism* (both published by Prentice-Hall as Spectrum Books). He is also the author of numerous articles on Soviet Communist Party history and foreign relations, and editor of volumes XIV–XVI of Stalin's *Sochineniia* (Works) in Russian.

International
Relations Among
Communists

edited by
ROBERT H. MCNEAL

Prentice-Hall, Inc.   A SPECTRUM BOOK   *Englewood Cliffs, N.J.*

To my parents

CONTENTS

The Soviet-Yugoslav Dispute

The Sino-Soviet Alliance

II
COMMONWEALTH
AND
CONFRONTATION, 1954–1960   72

Toward a De-Stalinized Order

The East European Crisis

Antirevisionism and the Quest for Unity

III

RIFT
AND
STALEMATE, 1961–1966   113

The Albanian Affair

Attempted Economic Integration

The Sino-Soviet Correspondence

By-Products and Aftermath
of the Sino-Soviet Encounter

The War in Vietnam
and the Sino-Soviet Stalemate

INTRODUCTION

As long as there have been nations there have been relations among them, but international relations among Communist parties and states have developed only recently. In embryo this category of international relations existed when the first network of fairly well organized socialist parties emerged about a century ago. But its mature form appeared only around the end of the Second World War, when a series of new Communist states were established alongside the Soviet Union, and the full flowering of the drama and difficulty inherent in international relations among Communists has occurred only in the last few years, the period of the Sino-Soviet dispute, among other problems.

Recent as it is, the existence of a separate category of international relations covering the intercourse among Communist parties and states is now well established and deserving of special study. Many books and articles on particular problems within this field have already appeared, but too little effort has been made to describe this peculiar system of international relations as a whole and to review its first generation of existence. In a small way this is what the present volume attempts to do, mainly by examining first-hand Communist documents on the subject. While it is true that Communists have been even more inclined than most political leaders to secrecy and deception and that a good deal of important information about their international relations is unknown to us, the body of documents that they have made public does represent a solid foundation for the study of international relations among Communists.

Because this book rests on the assumption that international relations among Communists are distinctive within the entire field of international relations, it is important to start with an appreciation of their peculiar characteristics. In general there are three kinds of special features that characterize these relations: ideological, institutional, and historical.

According to the Communists themselves, the foundation of their special international relationship is their common adherence to the *ideology* of Marxism-Leninism. And whatever one may say about the cynicism of Communist leaders in twisting ideology to suit their own aims, the fact remains that they have not yet come to the point of acknowledging that the internal political ideology of this or that country is irrelevant in international affairs.

However much they abuse one another they remain attached to the premise that history is moving toward the replacement of the capitalist socio-economic order with a socialist one, and that the countries possessing the new order *ought* to maintain a special, fraternal relationship among themselves —and with their cobelievers in countries that are still capitalist. Thus the deep-rooted assumptions that Communist leaders make about the nature of things stimulate a strong desire for unity and harmony in their international relations. Although the concluding appeal of the Communist Manifesto— "Working men of all countries, unite!"—provides no blueprint for unity, it and innumerable similar statements have given contemporary Communism a vital myth of worldwide unity. This has been a source of both strength and weakness, and is certainly a marked peculiarity of Communist international relations. There is enough sincere belief in this myth of unity to influence men's actions. At times it has been a useful tool for a dictator—notably Stalin, who aspired to maximize the obedience of all Communists to him. Even in times of open discord, the myth of unity inhibits Communists from ignoring entirely their relations with other Communists in order to achieve advantageous deals with non-Communists.

From the present perspective, however, it seems that the special role of ideology in international relations among Communists is less to provide real unity and strength than to aggravate the difficulties in achieving the desired goal. Because of their mutual adherence to a single creed—allegedly the one true revelation concerning all human affairs—Communists insist that their international harmony be based on an unrealistically high level of agreement on ideology. Moreover, the dogmatic approach that all Communist parties have built up concerning ideology, the tradition in each party of ruthlessly snuffing out "deviation," makes it almost impossible for them to tolerate disagreement in the world community of Communists. While non-Communist diplomats generally take it for granted that countries will differ in interest and outlook, Communists approach one another with a tendency to regard disagreement as heresy, betrayal. And their experience with ideology has provided them with a rich vocabulary of ideological epithets with which to insult, though scarcely to convince, their Communist adversaries.

The point is not that Communists were the first to introduce ideology into world politics. The attempts of Metternich in his day to base international harmony on generally conservative premises or the efforts of Woodrow Wilson to lead a community of states sharing a democratic ideology are cases in which ideology certainly played some role in international relations. But in non-Communist international experience ideology has rarely been regarded as dogma covering all branches of human affairs, and it has never before provided such unrealistically high expectations concerning unity in practice. The degree to which ideology is considered the foundation of international harmony is unique among Communists, as is the degree to which they regard differences of opinion as ideological betrayal. And no previous form of international relations saw ideology incarnate in special institutions that carry on international relations of their own, as do the Communist parties.

This brings us to the *institutional* feature of our subject: the party. While organizations that are called parties are active in a variety of countries, the Communist parties, along with a few now-defunct relatives such as the Nazis and Fascists, are something far different from the older, parliamentary-model parties. The Communist party is not intrinsically interested in parliamentary affairs or elections, but is a "movement"—or rather the would-be leadership of a movement—for the transformation of man and society. In countries that have wholly or predominantly Communist governments the party not only forms policy for the state but undertakes the supervision of the entire execution of policy and in many ways attempts to work directly in the administration and transformation of society. It is a kind of supergovernment, operating both above and beside the state itself. In countries where the Communists are not in power the party sets as its ultimate goal the replacement of the existing order with a party-regime of this sort. Whether it is in or out of power, each Communist party regards itself as the rightful arbiter of an unlimited range of human concerns.

Communists naturally consider international relations one of the party's areas of interest. In relations between a Communist country and a non-Communist country the party formulates broad policy, but does not actually carry out diplomatic transactions, because conventional governments usually abide by the understanding that they will conduct relations only with other governments, not with foreign parties. This conventional type of diplomatic relations usually exists between any two Communist countries as well. The diplomatic services of Communist countries have therefore grown up as branches of the respective states, directed by the party but not actually a part of it. Ambassadors are exchanged and interstate transactions take place in the normal ways. But above and beside these conventional diplomatic institutions the parties of the various Communist states usually carry on their own international relations. This represents a major institutional peculiarity in international relations among Communists, one with no significant historical precedent. This additive to conventional diplomatic institutions is still fairly new and has not yet evolved the kind of established rules that, for conventional diplomacy, are summarized in Satow's *Guide to Diplomatic Practice*. The very quest for a stable set of rules of the game, which provides one of the main issues among Communists and is a recurring

theme in this book, has created a problem of relations between parties that
is here to stay.

In relations between parties, at least one of which is *not* in power, there
can, of course, be relations only between parties. Most countries in the
world do not have Communist governments, so there are many Communist
parties not in power that nevertheless claim the right to participate in international transactions among Communists. Even the smallest Communist
party that has no real prospect of coming to power may carry on direct
relations with the mighty Communist Party of the Soviet Union or of China
—or with some other party that is not in power, such as the French Communist Party. The participation, in the international affairs of Communism,
of party organizations that direct no state is, then, another peculiarity of
the institutional character of our problem.*

It is a premise of this book that the mature stage of international relations among Communists was reached only when Communist parties had
come to power in several countries and the pattern of parallel state-to-state
and party-to-party relations emerged. But this mature system emerged
against a special *historical* background, which constitutes the third major
characteristic of international relations among Communists. The main
feature of this background is the unique and dominant position of the
Soviet Union during the generation preceding the appearance of a group of
such countries. The Bolshevik branch of the Russian Social Democratic
Workers' Party in 1917 became the first party of avowed followers of Marx
to rule a country, and until about 1945 it occupied this position in solitary
splendor.** The real power that the Soviet Communist party possessed
and the prestige that it enjoyed among Communists was so enormously
greater than that of any other national party that the history of international
relations among Communists is peculiarly preoccupied by the problem of
the relation of the U.S.S.R. to the Communist movements elsewhere. Until
1943 the predominance of the U.S.S.R. was symbolized by the Communist

* The three kinds of relationships involving Communists may be schematically
summarized thus:
Type 1: Between Communist country and non-Communist country—*only* interstate
relations are involved (e.g., U.S.S.R.-U.S.A.)
Type 2: Between Communist country and Communist country—interstate *and* inter-
party relations are involved (e.g., U.S.S.R.-China)
Type 3: Between Communist parties, at least one of which is *not* in power—*only*
interparty relations are involved (e.g., Communist Party of the Soviet Union
—Communist Party of France).
This book concerns both types 2 and 3.
** The People's Republic of Mongolia, founded in 1924, does not represent a
serious exception to this generalization.

International (Comintern), which the Soviet leaders controlled. For the next ten years the Soviet bloc of states in Europe and Asia—all ostensibly loyal to Moscow except for Yugoslavia after 1948—was the symbol of continuing Soviet predominance. Since 1953 the edifice of Soviet authority has crumbled, but the efforts to find a new form of ideologically-based unity have in large measure revolved around the historic legacy of Soviet predominance. Pre-Communist, conventional international relations evolved out of the European state system, in which no single power exercised hegemony, and the very institutions of Western diplomacy were shaped by repeated efforts to assure that no single state would achieve mastery. This historical background may help to explain why the theory of national sovereignty has had real and established meaning in conventional diplomacy and why a spirit of give-and-take has been identified with the professional diplomat. In international relations among Communists a contrasting heritage exists,—the legacy of Lenin's role as the spiritual founder of all existing Communist parties, of Soviet hegemony over other Communist parties, and of efforts by non-Soviet Communists to advance their sovereignty against this powerful center. But this book does not approach international relations among Communists as if it were only a question of "the Soviet-Yugoslav dispute," "the Soviet-Hungarian question," "the Sino-Soviet dispute," and similar bilateral affairs in which the Soviet Union represents one side. A broader, multilateral framework has come into existence and can be expected to develop further. And yet one must not forget the peculiar, Soviet-centered historical conditions in which international relations among Communists had their start.

THE HERITAGE OF THE THREE INTERNATIONALS

These historical conditions are part of a longer tradition of the world socialist movement that was embodied in the three "Internationals." Although there has been no really comparable organization since 1943—that is, during the period with which this book is concerned—some sketch of the history of the Internationals is necessary in order to appreciate the continuity of the myth of proletarian unity; for the strength of that myth to the present day is in part their legacy.

The first, or "International Working Men's Association," lasted only from 1864 to 1876. It was succeeded by the Second, or Socialist, International, which was founded in 1889, fundamentally damaged by the outbreak of war in 1914, and only weakly carried on by the parliamentary-socialist parties after that. For Lenin and Communists who organized themselves after the First World War the only true International became the Third, or Communist, International (Comintern), which was founded in Moscow in 1919 and was dissolved by its own decree in 1943. Although these three organizations differ in various important respects, all started with the socialist faith in the capacity of the working-class movement to overcome the old antagonisms among nations, to realize the watchword "fraternity" on a worldwide basis. All fell short of this goal, yet each established some form of international organization and contributed to the mythology of proletarian internationalism.

In the lifetime of Karl Marx socialist organizations were few and in their infancy, while the line of demarcation between socialism and other more or less radical movements was not clearly drawn. The First International began by inviting the democratic nationalist Mazzini to draft its program and ended its own existence partly out of fear that the anarchist and sometime panslavist Bakunin would gain control. Between these events Marx and his colleague Friedrich Engels succeeded in leading a series of "world congresses" and a standing body called the "general council," which at least represented a plausible starting point for international working-class fraternity. Despite the domineering personality of Marx, the First International helped to establish the assumption that this fraternity should be based on the preservation of the integrity of the various national "societies" (the word "party" was not yet in vogue among radicals) and that international agreement among socialists should be reached through democratic-parliamentary means.

This assumption was still prevalent among the growing socialist parties of Europe after Marx had died, and was embodied in the founding of the Second International in Paris in 1889. While the growth of socialist parties made it a more imposing organization than the First, this very advance made international integration more difficult, for the stronger individual parties became, the greater stake they acquired in defending their sovereignty. For this reason and because of the genuine democratism of most socialist leaders of the day, the Second International somewhat resembled the future League of Nations or United Nations in its lack of supranational authority. At the nine congresses that it held before 1914 decisions were not reached unless there was near-unanimity, and the general line of the loosely-united socialists remained quite vague. Despite the preponderance of avowed Marxists in the International there was little insistence on doctrinal agreement as a basis for world-wide socialist action. The non-Marxist Labour Party of Britain and Socialist-Revolutionary Party of Russia, as well as "revisionist" (avowed reformist) Marxists, were permitted to participate. On the vital question of unified tactics in defeating capitalism, especially in preventing capitalist states from starting wars, the International was able to produce only hopelessly vague formulations.

The efforts of a minority to deal with the issue of war somewhat resembled the later attempts of nonsocialist internationalists to organize machinery within the League of Nations or United Nations that would commit members to act with force on behalf of the world body against any breach of the peace. In the case of the socialists this meant commitment to some revolutionary plan of action, such as a general strike, that would paralyze the capitalist states. But as in the League and U.N. the majority of members of the Second International were not prepared to mortgage their sovereignty to prevent war. True, they did establish an International Socialist Bureau in 1901, but they endowed it only with consultative and coordinating responsibilities, not supranational authority. When war broke out in 1914 it became clear that the International lacked plans or organization that could work, and the majority of the "comrades" supported not internationalism but their bellicose fatherlands.

The catastrophe of the Second International, like the First World War itself, was a grievous blow to tolerance and democracy in Western civilization. The fiasco gave dogmatic, authoritarian Marxists like Lenin a matchless opportunity to associate "revisionism" and the whole of democratic socialism with "betrayal" of the interests of the masses. The cruel results of modern nationalism in the drawn-out war produced in some socialists such a strong revulsion against nationalism that they were willing to contemplate the organization of a new movement possessing unprecedented supranational authority. Lenin, by distinguishing himself for his attacks on the "imperialist war" and the "social patriots" who supported it, had laid the foundations for his moral authority among the left internationalists even before his return to Russia in 1917. His emergence at the head of the world's first avowedly Marxist government in November of that year made his prestige all the more powerful among the socialists who had lost patience with the Second International.

Such was the moral capital with which the Third International opened operations in 1919. Without this unique aura of prestige, Lenin could have hardly passed off its first congress in March of that year as anything more than a sham, for it consisted mainly of unrepresentative socialists who happened to be in Russia at the time. Nor could Lenin and his Soviet cohorts have succeeded at the second, much more representative world congress of 1920 in imposing 21 rigorous conditions for membership on all parties that wished to adhere to the Comintern. Previously international relations among socialist parties—at least the larger ones—had been based on a sense of equality, and no one party could dominate the others. But between approximately 1919 and 1945 the enormous prestige and power of Lenin's Bolshevik party stood in a class by itself, and it was simply impossible for international relations among Communist parties to be conducted on an equal footing. True, the statutes of the new organization failed to reflect this reality. According to these rules the Comintern was to operate on the basis of approximate equality among member parties. While the Comintern World Congress and the Executive Committee were to represent the parties of the great countries more heavily than the lesser ones, the Soviet party was not allocated a predominant share of votes. This was partly a reflection of the initial, optimistic expectation that the victory of workers' revolutions in a number of important countries would tend to equalize the real importance of the Soviet and other major parties. Germany was considered the greatest hope, and Lenin even spoke of transferring Comintern headquarters to Berlin after the revolution there. But the equity and parliamentary procedure that were formally embodied in the Comintern were increasingly subordinated in practice to centralized authority under Soviet control. Just as the procedures of democratic government were formally observed but in reality stifled within Lenin's Communist Party, they were also observed in the letter and stifled in the spirit within the Comintern. In fact, the same label—"democratic centralism"—that Lenin and his cohorts used to decorate their dictatorship within the Bolshevik party was also adopted in the International.

The centralized, supranational authority of the Comintern, dominated by the (Russian) Bolsheviks, replaced the older type of "international relations" among Communist parties. In place of separate national parties that treated one another as sovereign allies there was ideally only one "world party," in which national parties were formally called "sections of the Communist International." True, this ideal was not achieved at once, despite the prestige of Lenin. In 1921, at a meeting of Italian socialists who were considering acceptance of the Comintern system, the official representatives dispatched from Moscow were greeted with sarcastic cries of "Long live the Pope!" Years of struggle and maneuvering directed by the Moscow leadership (under G. E. Zinoviev until 1926) were needed to expel dissenters and whip the faithful into line. The considerable success that was achieved in this was made possible partly by the formation of a Comintern officer corps, recruited from the most obedient Communists of diverse nationality. The Italian Togliatti, the Hungarian Kun, the Bulgarian Dimitrov, the German Ulbricht, the Indian Roy, and the Yugoslav Broz (later called Tito) were among the determined Leninist-Stalinists who at one time or another between the world wars served in this foreign legion of the Bolshevik Party. They were indeed militant and militarized in their discipline before Soviet authority, making it possible for Moscow to staff the bureaucracy of the Comintern with reliable Communists from many lands. This greatly facilitated the ability of the Third International to appear truly international, rather than Soviet-dominated, and to send able representatives from its headquarters to diverse countries to supervise the activities of the national parties. Indeed, one of the primary institutions of the Comintern was the resident "rep" from Moscow who was usually present among the Communists of a given nation. Above these representatives stood resident regional directors, heading, for example, the West European or Asian "bureaus." Although these directors normally possessed command authority over the parties to which they were dispatched, it is in some ways helpful to think of them as a regular diplomatic service linking the Soviet Communist Party and other national parties. In this framework multilateral relations did not amount to much, but bilateral relations were highly developed.

The pattern of international relations among Communists that existed under the Comintern seemed fairly secure. The very fact that the Moscow leadership could call on foreign parties to follow policies that were against their local interests seemed to demonstrate solidarity. For example, Moscow ordered the young Chinese Communist Party to support Chiang Kaishek's Kuomintang, even after it had turned violently against the Communists; Moscow ordered the German Communists to oppose the Social Democrats with all possible force at the very time when only collaboration could have prevented Hitler from coming to power; Moscow ordered various European Communists to oppose the national resistance to the German threat after the signing of the Nazi-Soviet pact of 1939.

But how secure, in fact, was this international system? The unrequited sacrifices of the non-Soviet Communist parties depleted the moral capital with which Lenin had started the Comintern, and it must be kept in mind that worldwide unity and discipline was largely based on voluntary loyalty. To be sure, those foreign Communists who took up residence in the Soviet Union found in the 1930s that they were subject to the same cruel purges that Stalin wreaked on the Bolshevik party. And during the Spanish Civil War, which saw considerable numbers of non-Soviet Communists dispatched to participate in the defense of the Republic, Russian secret police, operating on Spanish soil, liquidated many of the Communist personnel. But by and large Stalin was limited in his use of physical force outside Soviet borders before the close of the Second World War. And we may surmise, on the basis of his whole career, that he did not like to depend on voluntary loyalty. He had nothing to say in public concerning his insecurity, but the transfer of the functions of Comintern executive apparatus to the secretariat of the Soviet Communist Party in 1937 indicated uneasiness. Another indication in his lack of explicit doctrinal statements on the subject. Stalin was not generally loquacious in public during his years of supreme authority, but he did on a number of highly glorified occasions deliver theoretical statements that were regarded as "classics of Marxism-Leninism." But in these statements the question of international relations among Communists never was mentioned in any specific and substantial way after the issue itself had emerged. This silence was perhaps most noticeable after the dissolution of the Comintern and the appearance of separate Communist states, but Stalin's unwillingness to commit himself on this matter goes back to the '30s. If there *was* a definite and specifically Stalinist doctrinal teaching that touched on international relations among Communists, it was surely the doctrine of "socialism in one country." Stalin conceived this view as an answer to his critics in the internal disputes of the Soviet Communist Party, but it seemed to have an implied meaning of broader import. In the doctrinal context in which Stalin presented it and in association with the rising official campaign of Russian nationalism in Stalin's mature years, "socialism in one country" may be perceived as a forerunner of the idea of "national Communism" or of "separate paths" to Communism. In his doctrine Stalin argued that Russia had a special path to Communism, based on special historical conditions, and in the revived, acute Russian nationalism of his dictatorship there seemed to be an assumption that this was a very Russian path indeed. True, Stalin may have meant that the Soviet path to Communism, while the product of special circumstances, provided a model that could be followed elsewhere—although he never made this point a clear dogma. And he may have meant that the greatness of Russian national culture should lead to its emulation and assimilation among all Communists. But seen through the eyes of at least some non-Soviet Communists, Stalin's teachings and policy on nationalism may have appeared as a license for various special national paths and for the adoption of one's own nationalism by Communists everywhere.

This must for the time being remain a matter for speculation. But there is some evidence that at least the Chinese Communists interpreted Stalinism along the lines mentioned. Here was a vigorous Communist Party based on an ancient and distinctive culture, armed and engaged in civil war from the 1920s onward, and not really integrated into the Comintern organization. Unlike industrialized Japan, whose socialists had participated directly in the Second International, unlike colonial countries in which native socialism had grown up in contact with the socialism of the ruling power (as in India or Indonesia), China stood outside the general stream of Marxism. Her self-taught Marxists, after organizing themselves in 1921, had only a short and disastrous experience under the tutelage of the Comintern. The Moscow-based organization had sent them advisers whose advice very nearly led to the destruction of the Chinese Communist Party in the later '20s, when Chiang turned harshly against it, and the survival of the party was more in spite of than because of Comintern assistance. The Chinese party thereafter had only weak ties with the Comintern system, either through participation in its central bodies or through the reception of representatives from Moscow. In 1935, the hardy, peasant-guerilla leader Mao Tse-tung was elected secretary of the party without the consent of Moscow, which was contrary to the practice that had by then become general. Mao avoided any public challenge to Stalin, but implied a declaration of independence by publishing from the late '20s onward peculiarly Maoist tracts on the organization of a rural base for "Marxist" revolution. Holding out in their mountain citadel of Yenan, to which they had retreated in 1934-35, the Chinese Communists in effect maintained a small, sovereign state that the capitalists could not reach and the Comintern could not subject to its discipline.

The Second World War threatened to weaken the pattern of direct control within the Comintern and to spawn other autonomous Communist areas. Communications were seriously weakened and in some European countries Communist-led guerilla forces, operating without Soviet help, emerged as possible candidates for postwar power. Tito established his "Yenan" in the Dinaric Alps and, as Togliatti noted in 1956, "the autonomy of these [European] parties became greater." The authority of Moscow was not challenged, however, and the kind of Communist leader that Stalin had approved in most parties demonstrated no desire to break discipline. But from Stalin's point of view the situation by the middle of the war must have seemed ominous for the old centralism. If discipline could not be enforced with full certainty (and Stalin was always hypersensitive on this point), could not the Comintern become a liability to his power? The non-Soviet Communist parties could all claim representation in the World Congress, and the larger parties had a claim on representation in the Executive Committee. If even a shadow of real independence were revived by autonomous Communist leaders within this machinery, what difficulties might ensue in these representative bodies of the Comintern?

We cannot be sure that Stalin had such questions in mind when he ordered the Presidium of the Executive Committee of the Communist International to declare the whole organization dissolved on May 15, 1943. But the usual explanation that he did this to please his capitalist allies will not bear examination. The fairly full published records of the wartime relations among Britain, the United States, and the Soviet Union do not reveal that the Western countries urged Stalin to make this concession.

What the documents do reveal is that Stalin was a tough negotiator who showed little concern for the sensibilities of the capitalists. The official declaration of the termination of the Comintern makes no mention of pleasing the capitalists, but, in its stress on national diversity, does hint that Stalin anticipated a breakdown of the old pattern of discipline.

This is not to argue that Stalin had lost interest in discipline. His relations with foreign Communists after the dissolution of the Comintern bear witness to this. But the old form of organization may have presented greater potential liabilities than assets, while a new pattern, based on bilateral relations between the Soviet party and the others, seemed more promising. In such a relationship the Soviet party might not always be able to exercise absolute authority, but at least the odds would be more favorable to it and the chances of anti-Soviet groupings among Communists would be reduced.

The end of the era of the three Internationals approximately coincided with the opening of the era of diverse Communist states and the mature form of international relations among Communists. In retrospect, the achievements of the three Internationals seem quite modest. In almost 80 years they failed to produce or even assist a single successful Communist revolution, nor did they bequeath a durable basis for international co-operation. Proclamatory unanimity was achieved among various socialists in the Internationals during the years when none of them held responsibility for governing, while the Comintern could provide unanimity based only on Soviet predominance. But no truly supranational authority was ever established, nor any principle of organization that did not rest on separate national parties. When the era of the Internationals ended, there was neither an organized community of sovereign parties nor the foundations of a "United States of the World," to use Lenin's optimistic label.

On the other hand, the Internationals provided a more definite framework for international relations than anything the Communists have had since. These organizations at least embodied some semblance of a formal standard of representation and a procedure for decision-making. Basically the framework was parliamentary in form, and it was probably for that very reason that Stalin discarded it. But the inability of the world's Communist parties—and not just Stalin—to accommodate themselves to a parliamentary framework has in the years since the Comintern proven to be a serious liability.

INTERPARTY RELATIONS

In the absence of a world organization to regulate the relations among Communist states and parties, it has been necessary for them to search for alternative bodies and procedures. This quest has not been particularly successful, and at different times various means of conducting relations have been emphasized. Still, some rough sketch of the institutions of Communist international relations in the years since the Comintern is both feasible and desirable as background for the study of the first-hand documents. In domestic affairs Communists have generally been able to integrate party and state institutions quite successfully, while in international relations the duality has proven confusing and burdensome. Still, it is a real duality, and our classification of the institutions of Communist international relations can usefully be based on a distinction between party and state.

Bilateral Relations

Bilateral relations between Communist parties have been more highly developed than multilateral relations since the dissolution of the Comintern. Even before 1943, as we have noted, the Soviet Union was fostering close bilateral relations between its party and those of foreign countries. Stalin continued this tendency in the latter years of his life, making considerable use of the relatively reliable corps of former Comintern bureaucrats who had lived for some time in the U.S.S.R. There was no general, multilateral organization of Communist parties, and Stalin discouraged any bilateral relations except those with his own Soviet party. Even before the condemnation of Tito in 1948, the Soviet leadership had reacted strongly against the close Tito-Dimitrov (Yugoslav-Bulgarian) relations that had begun to emerge. Only after Stalin did the Chinese really begin to develop foreign Communist-party relations (one exception is perhaps its ties with near neighbors, such as the Vietnamese Communists). After Stalin died, there was some revival of efforts to build multinational Communist relations, but bilateral relations still remained predominant because of the great difficulties that arose in the path of multilateral gatherings of a general or even a regional nature.

The definition of "party relations," as they are officially called, is not entirely clear. Unlike conventional diplomacy, there is no exchange of accredited representatives with published formalities, and at times it is not easy to know whether relations between any two given parties exist or not. Perhaps it is safe to say that relations between any two parties may exist unless there is some explicit statement to the contrary, such as the Cominform's condemnation of the Yugoslav Communist Party in 1948. Parties having mutual relations usually send representatives as observers at one another's party congresses, unless prevented by difficult conditions, as in the cases of some illegal parties that are barely surviving. Chinese and

Soviet relations at the time of the latter's party congress of 1966 illustrate the point. The Chinese were invited by the Soviets but contemptuously declined to attend, which seemed tantamount to a rupture of party-to-party relations.

When relations exist between parties that hold power in their home countries, the ambassadors exchanged between the states have not kept aloof from party affairs. In Stalin's day Soviet ambassadors in Eastern Europe resembled satraps, accepted as having ultimate authority on almost any question. In later years the ambassadors have played a more modest role in interparty relations, but have at least been the deliverers and recipients of messages, including some of the Sino-Soviet letters. To a large extent, however, bilateral relations between parties have been carried on by party officials who are not in the diplomatic service. Personal meetings at the summit of party authority have been fairly common among Communist leaders in power—and substantially more common than summit meetings in the world of conventional diplomacy. The relative frequency of such meetings may in fact reflect the absence of established machinery for international communication between Communist parties. Below the summit numerous special party delegations (sometimes combined "party-state" delegations) have been dispatched on bilateral missions. Generally the publicly announced consultations last only a few days. In addition to the publicized missions of this sort, which are possible within Communist countries and other countries that tolerate the presence of such emissaries, there have undoubtedly been many secret visits by representatives of one party to another. It appears that special interparty delegations have passed to or from the two great powers of Communism, the Soviet Union and China, more often than between the lesser parties, but there are many known cases of bilateral contact between such parties as the Italian and Yugoslav, Yugoslav and Hungarian, and French and Polish.

The larger and better established Communist parties, while they do not maintain regular "party ambassadors" to represent them with fraternal parties, do have special offices and personnel in the central apparatus to look after this work—a kind of Communist party foreign office. To a large extent the men who work in this specialty are quite a contrast to the state diplomats, who tend to be technicians in a nonideological profession. The experts in party relations, on the other hand, are not only full-time employees of the party, but are also specialists in matters of ideology. This is particularly true in the Soviet party, which maintains a special office under the Central Committee to deal with international relations among Communists. For a number of years preceding his death in 1948, A. A. Zhdanov, who was probably Stalin's most intently ideological henchman, seems to have run this department. Subsequently M. A. Suslov, also regarded as a devout ideologist, appears to have been the nearest thing to a "foreign secretary of the Communist Party of the Soviet Union." On the Chinese side it appears that an old party hand and colleague of Mao Tsetung, Liu Shao-chi, played this role. In any case, the personnel carrying on relations with other Communist parties are men whose careers and experience make the search for ideological orthodoxy much more natural than the spirit of compromise. The ideological character of international relations among Communists may have made it inevitable that such men represent their parties, but it appears likely that their very personalities and habits of conduct have been detrimental to the amicable settlement of interparty differences.

Multilateral Relations

The multilateral institutions of Communist international relations deserve careful attention even though their significance derives more from their failures or unrealized potential than from their accomplishments. In view of the strong myth of fraternal internationalism, world-wide party unity has never ceased to be a major aspiration, presumably in some organized form. There is no specific name for the most comprehensive Communist international body, but its model was the conference of 81 parties that met in Moscow in 1960. A fairly elaborate affair convened by the Soviet party, the conference was preceded by a preparatory session of representatives from all the major parties except Yugoslavia's. Khrushchev no doubt regarded this as the correct pattern for the integration of Communism on the highest international plane, and in 1964 attempted to arrange a similar meeting. Another preliminary drafting session of 26 major parties was called for, but before it could meet Khrushchev was forced into retirement and the session postponed. When it finally met in March, 1965, attended by only 17 parties, it was called merely a "consultative meeting" and was followed by no major international convention. While a number of parties continued to maintain afterward that they regarded some such general meeting as the supreme form of Communist international relations, its revival faced great difficulties. At no time were the fundamental questions of power and representation solved with regard to the general meeting. No real voting was possible because there was no agreement on the complex question of satisfying the claims of such diverse parties as the Soviet, the Albanian, the Indonesian, and the Costa Rican. The absence of some accepted procedure for settling disputes and reaching decisions in effect deprived the 1960 conference of much power beyond the pronouncement of generalities, and no legitimate basis for enforcing the "decisions" of the conference was ever established. The further development of the Sino-Soviet quarrel pretty well assured that there would either be no further general meetings, or that such gatherings would be general in name only, and would actually represent only the Soviet or Chinese factions. No standing secretariat or similar office was created by the 1960 conference, and Soviet interest in such a step, expressed from time to time, has met with frustration.

The next lower level of multilateral Communist international organization is the meeting of representatives of parties that hold power in their respective countries. This form of organization, met formally only in November, 1957, on the occasion of the fortieth anniversary of the Bolshevik revolution, and consisted of only 13 parties. As in the conference of 81 parties, no definite principle of procedure was established and no authority was established that could oblige the Yugoslav representatives to sign the rather general declaration of the meeting, which they considered hostile to their interests. The conference did succeed in establishing a general Communist organ, the *World Marxist Review* (*Problems of Peace and Socialism* in its Russian edition). Harking back to the various publications of the Comintern, such as *International Press Correspondence,* the new periodical at first provided a forum for and coverage of Communist parties in and out of power. But its editorial board was controlled by the Soviets, and in the era of the Sino-Soviet rift the *World Marxist Review* became a partisan organ that could only exacerbate the issues between the disputants. The Chinese withdrew from its editorial board in 1963. Multilateral meetings of representatives of the parties in power have met in various other guises, which are noted below (e.g., gatherings of foreign guests at the congresses of individual national parties), but no special conference of parties in power has emerged as an institution.

Stalin attempted to establish a regular organization of representatives of nine parties, including seven that held power, called the Communist Information Bureau (Cominform). This institution, founded in 1947, showed intermittent signs of vitality. A meeting of leading European Communists, including Zhdanov and Malenkov from the Soviet Union, proclaimed its existence in 1947, and in 1948 and 1949 major sessions of the body for the purpose of castigating the Yugoslav leadership were attended by important Communists. In 1951, Stalin invited Togliatti to become Secretary-General of the Cominform, a post that had not existed before and was never filled. But the regular membership of the Bureau consisted of distinctly third-rate party bureaucrats (two from each member party), and the only significant activity of the body, excepting the special meetings noted above, was the publication of a Soviet-dominated newspaper, absurdly called *For a Lasting Peace, For a People's Democracy!* The exclusion of the Chinese Communist Party from the Cominform was another clear mark of its weakness, and it was abandoned in 1956 to please Tito, whom it had persecuted so loudly and uselessly.

A fairly informal but quite flexible institution of international relations among Communists is the congress of an individual national party, especially a party in power. The party congress is essentially a domestic affair, a gathering of representatives, supposedly elected by the lower ranks of the party, which generally meets every few years to hear reports from the leaders and to approve the general policy line. Its international role derives from the customary attendance of observers from fraternal parties. These have no vote in the proceedings of the host party, but they may take advantage of the assembly to discuss matters of common interest with representatives from other national parties, and they may have a chance to deliver a speech to the congress. The importance of this medium of communication grew from the early postwar years until the early 1960s, when Khrushchev pressed too hard to use Rumanian, Soviet, and East German party congresses to his advantage in the dispute with the Chinese. In the case of the Rumanian congress of 1960 the visiting representatives were unexpectedly assembled under Khrushchev's leadership to form an improvised general conference of party representatives, which a Soviet textbook on international relations regards as roughly equivalent in stature to the general conference that met in Moscow later in the same year. The Chinese, not expecting this maneuver, were at a disadvantage in that their delegation was headed by the second-rank official P'eng Chen, while Khrushchev himself led the Soviet group. The Chinese again found themselves at a disadvantage at the Soviet party congress in 1961. Although represented by Premier Chou En-lai, they could not interfere with the Soviet management of the agenda, including sharp attacks on Stalin (whose corpse was removed from the Lenin mausoleum) and on the Albanian friends of China. This led to a Chinese walkout before the end of the congress, a clear sign that it had failed as a medium of negotiation. In 1963, the Soviets directed an effort to humiliate Chinese and Chinese-supporting visitors to the East German party congress by drowning their orations in a din of whistles and foot-stamping but this merely undermined the national party congress as a medium of international relations. Not only the Chinese but also other parties have become suspicious of what the host party (or its great-power patron) may spring on them in a relatively public forum. It appears that the Soviets were able to arrange the attendance at their party congress in 1966 of over 70 foreign delegations (not including the Chinese) only by agreeing to avoid direct or extended treatment of the most pressing international issues within Communism.

There is no obvious reason why there should not be frequent *ad hoc* multilateral conferences of party representatives, but in fact these seem to be fairly rare. Between 1957 and 1962 there were perhaps seven such gatherings, five of which were restricted to parties in power, four of these five explicitly related to the main Communist interstate organizations, the Council for Mutual Economic Assistance and the Warsaw Treaty Organization. In 1959 there were two meetings of the nonruling European Communist parties, one consisting of all 17 of these, the other merely of the parties in Common Market countries. But such gatherings have yet to become frequent or important. Before and after these years there have been fairly few overt, multilateral party gatherings; and in general such meetings do not appear to occur without the participation of the Soviet Union. This seems to be a legacy of the Stalinist discouragement of any form of independent grouping among the vassal parties.

Relatively low-level party representatives meet quite often at sessions of such Communist "front" organizations as the World Federation of Trade Unions, the World Peace Council, and the Afro-Asian Solidarity Conference. Because these gatherings include not only Communists but also various sympathetic "anti-imperialists" of one sort or another, they can scarcely assert any authority over the Communist leaders, who attempt to manipulate such bodies merely to influence non-Communist opinion. But they do provide a multilateral forum at which various Communist parties can contact or propagandize one another. The use of these meetings for such purposes grew up in the 1960s, wholly as a maneuver in the Sino-Soviet dispute, and the main result seems to have been to lower the prestige of the Communists in the eyes of the non-Communists present. In January, 1966, such problems beset the Tricontinental Solidarity Conference, meeting as the guests of Fidel Castro in Havana in an attempt to upgrade the Afro-Asian Solidarity Conference by the addition of Latin Americans and by the establishment of a permanent secretariat. The Soviet Union opposed this kind of institutional development unsuccessfully in the face of Cuban and Chinese arguments, and the latter two parties soon parted company over public Cuban charges that the Chinese were carrying out propaganda within the Cuban armed forces. Hence the prospects for organized solidarity in this form seem beclouded by a variety of problems.

Reviewing the experience of the past generation, it appears that no satisfactory system of world-wide interparty relations has been evolved by Communists. The Leninist-model party has been a great asset to Communists in the domestic politics of various countries as a means of gaining and holding power, but the insistence of the party on conducting special international relations has been on balance a liability.

INTERSTATE RELATIONS

There are 14 Communist states—that is, countries in which Communist parties hold power: Albania, Bulgaria, China, Cuba, Czechoslovakia, East Germany, Hungary, Mongolia, North Korea, North Vietnam, Poland, Rumania, the Soviet Union, and Yugoslavia. Because these parties maintain legally sovereign states, they are in a position to carry on conventional diplomatic relations among themselves, bilaterally and multilaterally.

Bilateral Relations

A perplexing and unresolved question concerning bilateral (state) relations between Communist countries is the extent to which these relations are different from diplomatic relations between capitalist countries or between communist and capitalist countries. Communist spokesmen have advanced a fairly elaborate theoretical argument to the effect that relations between their states are based on "new principles" that should lead to unprecedented harmony. These principles include "socialist internationalism" (essentially the old ideal expressed in the slogan "working men of all countries, unite!"), "the absence of antagonistic contradictions" (neither class struggle nor "imperialist" struggle for profits), the "popularity" of Communist foreign policy (the allegedly consistent support of peace by Communist states), and "the leading role of Communist and workers' parties" in the relations between Communist states. This optimistic picture of fraternal solidarity does not, however, specify any really new institutions or procedures in relations between states, except for the varieties of interparty relations that we have discussed. Nor does it cast much light on the problem of what Communist diplomats can do when disputes *do* arise, disputes which may be acute, even if they are supposedly "nonantagonistic." One might think that the diplomats could refer the more thorny problems to the party leaders, who are supposedly in fraternal relations around the world and who certainly have greater authority than the professional diplomats. Unfortunately, it seems to be precisely the party leaders who have the least ability to sit down with one another and work out their problems in a reasonable way. It is they, and not the diplomats, who hurl abuse at one another and on occasion find it impossible to even be in the same room together. Instead of referring disputes up the ladder of authority to the party bosses, the tendency in cases of conflict is to isolate conventional diplomatic relations from party relations and to leave it to the professional diplomats to keep up at least minimal, conventional relations. Thus the

Eastern European Communist states, including the Soviet Union, maintained formal diplomatic relations with heretical Yugoslavia right through the worst phase of the interparty dispute. True, the Cominform countries withdrew their ambassadors from Belgrade as a threatening gesture, and the Bulgarian foreign office was forced to disavow its initial statement that the ideological quarrel "in no way alters the existing friendly relations" between Bulgaria and Yugoslavia. But the virtual state of war between the Yugoslav and other Communist parties was not matched by a complete rupture in diplomatic relations between the states. A somewhat similar practice emerged by 1966 in Sino-Soviet relations. It was reported that the Soviet and other East European ambassadors to Peking were not actually on duty there and that consular representation was sharply cut back, but diplomatic relations between the states remained even after the Chinese had organized demonstrations in the street leading to the Soviet embassy, which was officially renamed "Struggle-against-Revisionism Street," a new kind of diplomatic slur. On the other hand, the Soviets alleged that the Albanian government had given sufficient pretext for the withdrawal of all Soviet diplomatic representation in Tirana, although other East European Communists states did not join in this action.

Whatever attempts have been made to segregate interstate from interparty relations, no serious interparty quarrel has failed to affect interstate relations. The Chinese and Soviet parties expressed dismay that their interparty conflict was "extended" or "transferred" to the sphere of state relations, but this should scarcely come as a surprise to party leaders who have consistently regarded the state as a mere instrument of the party.

Disputes between Communist countries often raise the question of noninterference in one another's internal affairs, which is supposed to be a principle of conventional international relations and has been recognized verbally by numerous Communist statements. In diplomatic practice embassies and consulates are not supposed to meddle in the domestic affairs of countries to which they are accredited. However, the "fraternal" concept of relations among Communists suggests a basis for concern by all Communists for the well-being of all their comrades, including the health of their theoretical views and practical programs. It is not difficult to disguise harsh intervention as comradely concern for the prevention of heresy. Even the small parties have come to claim a legitimate interest in the internal programs and policies of other parties—and why not, if sufficient error can convert a former member of the socialist camp into a capitalist opponent, as has been sometimes alleged? The tendency to segregate conventional diplomacy and its institutions from party quarrels has not gone so far that Communist embassies are consistently "correct" in their attitude toward the internal affairs of the country to which they are accredited. As previously observed, Soviet embassies in Eastern Europe under Stalin played a major role in directing the Communist parties there. In a letter to the errant Yugoslavs in 1948, Stalin made it clear that he did not consider ambassadors between Communist countries bound by the normal rules of "bourgeois" diplomacy when it came to the internal affairs of the countries in which they were stationed. "By being made an ambassador, he does not cease being a Communist," stated the Soviet note. By the 1960s the Soviets had toned down their violations of diplomatic conduct in this regard, but got some of their old medicine from the Chinese comrades (and the Albanians, too), who used their Moscow Embassy—a large, new building in an extensive private park—as a base for the manufacture and dissemination of propaganda attacking the "heretical" Soviet position in world affairs. The Chinese stoutly maintained that they had the right and duty to preach the truth to all proletarians.

At times the violation of the sovereignty of one Communist state by another in the name of ideological purity has involved devices other than diplomatic institutions. Radio stations operating in the language of the "deviant" country may be maintained on the soil of another Communist country, calling on the populace, and especially "true" Communists, to disobey their national party and state, or even to overthrow it. Printed tracts, introduced into the "deviant" country may serve the same purpose, and organizations of citizens of the "deviant" country in emigration may be supported as a thinly-veiled threat to form a government-in-exile. Tito's Yugoslavia received the full treatment, being the object of varied subversive, Soviet-sponsored activities in several Eastern European Communist states, including the Moscow-based newspaper *For a Socialist Yugoslavia,* which set the tone for the campaign. Some of these techniques were later revived against heretical Albania. All of this is reminiscent of Western, chiefly American-sponsored, efforts to undermine Communist governments by means of radio stations, printed matter, and subsidized émigré societies— and the futility of such activities in unseating any single Communist government is notably the same, whether the backer of the campaign has been Soviet or American. The Sino-Soviet quarrel has produced no such major campaign, but there have been violations of strict sovereignty in bilateral relations through means other than diplomatic representation. The Soviets presumably connived with an internal opponent of Mao, Marshal P'eng Teh-haui, in 1959, while the Chinese have used train crews on the Moscow-Peking run to distribute leaflets (to the sleepy Soviet peasants tending their cows on the right-of-way?).

So far there has never been a declared war by one Communist state against another. In view of the catastrophic role of war in international relations as a whole, this might be considered a major accomplishment of Communists, but such a laudatory conclusion must be tempered by several reservations. One is that there has been armed conflict in the form of border incidents at least between Yugoslavia and her Communist neighbors, in the days of Stalin, and on the Sino-Soviet frontier more recently. Still more serious was the assault by Soviet divisions against the Hungarian government of Imre Nagy in 1956. True, Nagy wished to withdraw his country from the Warsaw Treaty and to permit genuine domestic political pluralism, but he remained a Communist in his own eyes, and the government that the Red Army crushed was still Communist-led, even though supported by some non-Communists. The official Soviet view holds that the intervention was at the legitimate request of the *real* Communist government of Janos Kadar, but this merely demonstrates that any Communist government can be expected to proclaim that its adversaries in battle are traitors to the cause. Pretexts for such proclamations can always be discovered when and if it comes to war between Communists. Clearly peace among Communists thus far has been not a result of fraternal institutions nor any talent for conciliation, but rather of the *pax Sovietica* within much of the Communist world and fear of Cold War adversaries outside it.

Despite the complications of Communist bilateral diplomacy, many items of business between their states have been more or less successfully transacted, often by the negotiation of bilateral and other agreements. Because of the totalitarian nature of Communist governments, in which all types of human activities and institutions are subordinated to the party-state regime, the diplomatic services of Communist states indeed have a large and complex task to perform. Whereas it is not necessary for the British and American governments to arrange for the sale of Hollywood film-rights in Britain or the importation of Scotch whiskey into the United States, such mundane operations necessarily involve governments when Communist countries are involved. Just as the government has taken over the administration of the national economy, cultural life, medical services, and so on, the diplomatic representatives of the government must manage the international contacts and exchanges of all manner of institutions, including those that are autonomous in most non-Communist countries. Because of this situation it is probably safe to say that as a whole the relations between individuals and institutions in separate Communist countries are impoverished, that the "total international intercourse" (meaning the immeasurable mass of all forms of contact and exchange) is abnormally low. Despite all Communist theoretical claims that they have established new and higher forms of cooperation among nations, it seems undoubtedly true that, for example, the international intercourse between people and institutions in the United States and Canada or between France and Italy is vastly more than the international intercourse between the U.S.S.R. and Poland, not to speak of the U.S.S.R. and China. One rough index of this scarcely measurable factor might be the number of persons who cross between one country and the other. Only incomplete statistical comparison of even this limited point is possible, due to the absence of data from the Communist side, but anyone with the slightest familiarity with the question will agree that there is a tremendous impoverishment of Communist exchange of persons per year as compared to border-crossings among non-Communists.*

But if the totalitarian character of Communism limits the extent of international intercourse between Communist states, the diplomats have still managed to get through quite a lot of formal, bilateral business over the years. By 1957, the U.S.S.R. alone had over 600 publicly known agreements with other Communist states, of which 118 were concluded in 1957, showing an increased tempo in diplomatic transactions. The most exalted form that bilateral business has taken is the signing of about 30 treaties of "Friendship, Aid and Mutual Assistance," which began with the treaty between the U.S.S.R. and the then-non-Communist Czechoslovak government-in-exile in 1943. The fact that such treaties could be basically similar whether or not both partners are Communist illustrates well the lack of any new form of higher harmony that is specifically Communist. The friendship treaties are effusive as expressions of good will, but poor as even verbal defensive instruments, for they provide for a *causus foederis* only against aggression by defeated Germany and Japan and their anonymous allies. Granted that Japan is hardly likely to "attack" Communist China without the United States as an ally, it surely would be more reassuring to China to see the United States named, or covered in a blanket phrasing, as the "aggressor" against whom Russia would join China. As matters stand under the Sino-Soviet friendship treaty of 1950, which is typical of other inter-Communist bilateral pacts in form, the United States could by itself or in alliance with any country except Japan "attack" China without necessarily involving the U.S.S.R., which in any case preserves the right to define aggression as it wishes.

Another cluster of bilateral treaties, which was not so exalted but was more important in reality, consists of agreements regulating the status of Soviet military forces in Poland, East Germany, Hungary, and Rumania, all coming into force in 1957 in the wake of the disturbances of the autumn of

* For example, in 1963, 2.9 million Frenchmen went to Italy and 470,000 Italians went to France, while only 31,000 Soviet citizens went to Poland and 122,000 Poles went to the U.S.S.R. (reference is to visits, not migration). (United Nations, *Statistical Yearbook 1964* (New York, 1964), p. 432f.)

1956. It would be naïve to suppose that these verbal undertakings can really control Soviet military action in all contingencies, but the treaties no doubt reflected real inhibitions that renascent Eastern European national sovereignty could impose on the Soviets, and which the latter were willing to accept. The published terms varied somewhat, but the Polish-Soviet treaty, which was the most favorable of the lot, gave the host government major veto powers over the disposition and use of Soviet troops in the country.

Many of the agreements concluded between Communist governments are specifically connected with the state-operated economies, such as trade, barter, and aid agreements. The establishment of consular relations by special agreement is intended to facilitate such economic connections. Other agreements cover scientific and cultural exchange, mutual medical assistance, citizenship law, and legal aid. Considering that Communist countries have usually traded more among themselves than with outside countries and considering the bureaucratic difficulties that any Communist transaction is likely to involve, it seems safe to say that the professional diplomats have been very active and effective. But there is no reason to consider them unusually skilled at resolving conflicts and promoting international fraternity.

Indeed, their finest technical handiwork has proven highly vulnerable to party politics beyond the control of the diplomats. While it would be going too far to suggest that Communists can never trust one another to honor bilateral commitments, it must be acknowledged that the peculiar role of the party and of ideology in the background of Communist diplomacy complicates the problem of fulfilling agreements. Numerous examples of denounced or violated treaties and other agreements between Communist countries could be cited. The Yugoslavs in their dispute with Stalin's Soviet Union complained bitterly that the Soviets and their cohorts renounced existing treaties of friendship, aid, and mutual assistance, as well as other agreements. For their part, the Yugoslavs took the initiative in renouncing a similar treaty with Albania. All the renouncers proclaimed the extremity of the provocations that justified their action, which in all cases boiled down to ideological and party matters. In later years the most flagrant violation of an agreement was the Soviet withdrawal of technical aid to China in 1960, which aggrieved the Chinese mightily. This did not deter them from defaulting on rice shipments that they had agreed to send Cuba in 1966 (according to the Cuban version). Here again, the interparty disputes, and especially Cuba's increasingly antagonistic attitude toward Chinese tactics in the Sino-Soviet dispute, evidently explains the demise of the interstate agreement. In short, Communist states have no monopoly on dishonored

international agreements, but their peculiarly Communist character seems
to intensify rather than alleviate this old problem.

Multilateral Relations

Nor can Communist states point to any special accomplishments in the
field of multilateral interstate relations. At no time since the establishment
of multiple Communist states has there been any multilateral organization
embracing *all* of them. Such multilateral state organizations as have existed
among Communists have been predominantly European and Soviet-oriented.
By all odds the most important of these are the Council for Mutual Economic Assistance (CMEA—often referred to in the West as Comecon) and
the Warsaw Treaty Organization. The latter is essentially military, providing a Soviet commander-in-chief in practice and a joint military command
in theory, which has so far remained a dead letter. The organization has
political potentialities thanks to its Political Consultative Committee, which
is supposed to meet every six months and to form a standing secretariat.
These potentialities have remained largely latent. At times years have
elapsed between meetings of the Committee, which have usually been only
a day or so in duration, and the secretariat seems to be moribund. Comecon
is fundamentally devoted to the coordination of the economies of the member states, which is a highly political function in a Communist framework.
The Council itself, composed of high-level officials, has been fairly active,
meeting once or twice a year since Stalin's death to discuss high-level policy.
The Executive Committee of Comecon, added in 1962 and consisting of
deputy prime ministers, has met every few months and is more oriented to
economic matters, but is politically significant because it is the nearest thing
to supranational authority among Communists. The standing commissions
of Comecon deal with such technical fields as ferrous metallurgy and transport and are therefore less important to large considerations of power.

Both these multilateral bodies—Comecon and the Warsaw Treaty Organization—were formed as reactions to Western, non-Communist international actions, which may suggest that, left to their own devices, the
Communist states would have an even more paltry record in this area of
organization than is actually the case. Comecon was founded in 1949 as a
rather feeble response to the Marshall Plan, and has become more active
and pretentious partly in reaction to the flowering of the European Common Market. The Warsaw Treaty Organization was founded in 1954 in
response to the proposed European Defense Community, a plan for non-
Communist military unity that the United States supported and France
rejected. Since the Soviet Army had equipped, trained, and virtually controlled most of the Eastern European Communist armed forces before the

Warsaw Treaty, this organization represented a rather modest advance of real unity and at the same time has had a fairly stable existence. The hard core of Soviet-oriented Eastern European states have evidently been willing to continue close military collaboration with the Red Army. However, this core has been diminished by the defection of Albania in 1961, leaving Bulgaria, Czechoslovakia, East Germany, Hungary, Poland, Rumania, and the U.S.S.R. Efforts to bring in the Chinese, and with them the North Koreans and North Vietnamese, collapsed. These states participated as observers in meetings of the Warsaw Treaty Organization's political auxiliary bodies through 1961, when they, too, moved wholly out of the organization. Yugoslavia, holding a brief for military non-alignment, has never participated in the Soviet-dominated military organization. By 1966 Rumanian criticism of the Warsaw Treaty Organization raised the very question of its continued existence.

The future of Comecon seems more secure, at least in a limited area, and in the last ten years has had some real achievements. Stalin directed Soviet domination of satellite economics with relatively little multilateral integration, making Comecon a more or less stillborn body. His successors and the Eastern European leaders sought to change this and to develop a truly multilateral, fairly authoritative body, and in some measure they have succeeded. Its charter (1960) provided a constitutional basis for the organization for the first time. Between 1956 and 1963 twenty-two standing commissions dealing with such special areas as agriculture and atomic energy for peaceful uses were established, with headquarters for them distributed from Berlin to Ulan Bator. In 1964 an International Bank of Economic Cooperation began operations in an attempt to improve the integration of the pricing and accounting system for international trade among members. In 1966 an imposing building in Moscow was under construction as the permanent headquarters of Comecon, but it seemed unlikely that the organization would achieve much importance beyond a relatively narrow circle of the more economically developed Communist countries (the U.S.S.R., Poland, Czechoslovakia, East Germany, Hungary, along with comparatively less industrialized Bulgaria and Mongolia). There were efforts to integrate the Asian Communist countries, all of which were relatively unindustrialized: China, North Vietnam, and North Korea participated as observers and may have been offered full membership, quite possibly at an executive Committee meeting in October, 1963. But since the warming of the Sino-Soviet dispute in 1961 they have maintained only sporadic connections with Comecon. Yugoslavia, fairly unindustrialized in comparison with other European states, held observer status from 1956 to 1958, when political hostility led to a cessation of invitations. After relations with the Soviet Union had improved the Yugoslavs approached Comecon in 1961, but were faced with a choice of full membership, which probably seemed a risky commitment of sovereignty, or nothing, which was their choice. In the same year Albania, which is still less developed, quit or was ejected (it is a little hard to determine which) from the organization. But the most serious instance of discord between the more industrialized Comecon members and a less developed Communist state was that involving Rumania. Because the efforts to establish the supranational planning authority that Khrushchev put forward in 1962 involved de-emphasis of industry in favor of agriculture and the extraction of raw materials in Rumania, the Communist leadership there turned decisively against the new attempts at integration, seriously disrupting the plans of the Soviet Union and the other Comecon members. The international integration of socialist economies seems to have proven difficult, and the harmonization of the interests of industrialized and less developed Communist countries an insoluble problem.

Considering the whole complex of interparty and interstate relations between Communists, one can scarcely conclude that they possess, or are developing, new institutions of international relations that are superior to traditional ones. One might even say that they have failed to reach the level of the United Nations or Common Market, and in some respects fall below the standards of diplomatic technique that have been followed for centuries.

ISSUES BETWEEN COMMUNISTS

Although this book is based on the belief that the best introduction to the issues between Communist parties and states lies in primary documents, some remarks on the general nature of these issues are useful as an overture. Because the distinctive feature of Communist international relations is the common ideological premises of the participants, it is first important to decide how one is to perceive this dimension of the subject.

The Role of Ideology

All too often this question is approached as one of "theory *or* power," a matter of deciding whether Communists form and execute their policies as a sincerely attempted enactment of Marxist theory or, on the contrary, cynically seek power alone under the camouflage of Marxism. The latter approach may purport to be hard-headed, but is in truth deceived by its underestimation of the Marxian preoccupation with power, its acquisition and maintenance. There is no need for a Marxist-Leninist to choose theory *or* power. For him, that theory is most truly Marxist which contributes most to the acquisition and maintenance of Communist power. External critics of Communism may see matters differently and accuse Communists of distorting old doctrines in the name of expediency, but the Communist decision-makers will never acknowledge that this is the case, and in a sense they are right. Stalin once said that if Engels could see the Soviet Union he would say, "To the devil with all old formulas, long live the victorious revolution in the U.S.S.R.!," not meaning that theory was itself irrelevant, but that the essence of Marxian theory was Communist power.

Just as Communists assume an identification of the interests of power and ideology, they also assume an identification of the interests of the universalist ideological movement and the separate national Communist parties. Here again the external critic may see matters differently, but there is no reason to think that he can make the Communist of a given nation admit that his national interests clash with those of the international ideology. The Soviet Union in the era of the Comintern laid a solid foundation for this dogmatic outlook by representing itself as the bastion of all proletarian revolution, the interests of which were necessarily those of the world movement. For a generation Communists were taught to see one particular national interest, Soviet, as the interest of all, and it is not surprising that the next generation, which saw the appearance of other revolutionary bastions, should proclaim the identification of various national interests with the universal cause. This insistence on identity of national and ideological interests has been a powerful corrosive in relations among Communists since 1943. No party to a dispute will even admit that its own national interest *may* run counter to the universal interest of the ideology, but with the coming of increasing autonomy of parties there is an increasing number of spokesmen who are willing to find such a conflict of interest on the part of their Communist opponents. Thus the Soviet, Chinese, Yugoslav, Albanian, and other parties have at one time or another hurled charges of nationalism at their ideological adversaries and have been repaid in kind. The external observer may find the exchanges hypocritical, but the Communist is blinded to the obvious by his ingrained assumption that the national interest of *his* Communist party coincides with that of the international ideological movement.

In short, it is misleading to attempt to perceive the role of ideology as an alternative to considerations of power or national interest. Ideology is neither an external, dominating force nor a mere cloak for the "real" issues. It is more like a set of assumptions about the nature of the world and its problems, which is inextricably involved in Communist international issues as a conceptual framework or, more simply, as the language used to discuss these issues. International relations among Communists are not conducted in any *lingua franca* in the usual sense. Despite the importance of Russian, that language has not attained significant status outside Eastern Europe, and in 1964 the Chinese and Russians had a sharp exchange over the meaning of "request" and "demand" in Chinese, the language that the Peking regime insisted on using in its letters. Ideology does, however, supply a special kind of *lingua franca,* a vocabulary that transmits through connotation a set of values and that inhibits the flexibility of Communist thinking about international relations. It is obvious, for example, that "imperialism" has a connotation of evil as used by Communists. If something is "imperialist" there is no need to explain *why* it is inimical to righteousness. Because of their common indoctrination in Lenin's teachings, Communists automatically understand "imperialism" as "The Enemy," and it is really unnecessary to make any clear connection between the term and empires or international banking. It is equally obvious that anything called "democratic," "popular," or "fraternal" is good and needs no further argument on its behalf. To the outsider it may be somewhat less obvious that "nationalist" and "revisionist" are by definition bad, when the very Communists who use the terms as insults seem to be quite devoted to their own country and willing to admit that Marxism must be adapted to changing conditions. But these consider themselves "patriotic" and are avoiding the error of "dogmatism," according to the international language of Communism. Thus a "reading knowledge" of Communist ideological language is essential to a comprehension of the fundamental documents on the subject of this book.*

Communists' reliance on this special language affects not only their modes of communication but also their fundamental perception and analysis of the "imperialist" enemy and of each other. To some extent this may be helpful to them: It has been suggested, for instance, that ideological language provides Communist policy-makers with a conceptual tool that gives their strategy a consistency and a sense for power that is often lacking in less ideological countries. In Communist writings this advantage is exalted as "the true compass of Marxism-Leninism." There may be something to this with respect to such problems as strategy in the former colonial countries. Here the assumptions of Communist ideology at least tend to place Communism on the highly popular anticolonial side, for example. But with respect to international relations among Communists it seems that reliance on ideological language is far from advantageous. The tendency of Communists to treat language in a highly dogmatic way aggravates the international problems that exist in any case. More than most men, Communists

---

* For the same reason, a highly desirable introduction to Marxism-Leninism is R. N. C. Hunt's *The Theory and Practice of Communism* (New York, 1963). The same author has an introduction to the more specifically linguistic problem: *A Guide to Communist Jargon* (New York, 1957).

tend to mistake verbal assertion for actuality, to accept myths rooted in approved ideological language. This means that grave complications arise whenever a supreme arbiter is absent. It is all very well within one national Communist party to assert that perfect unity exists, for this pleasing myth can be superficially maintained by force. But on the international scene it is merely self-deluding to proclaim that the Communist parties of the world enjoy a "fraternal" relationship. If the use of such a word in the official statements of the Communist conferences of 1957 and 1960 were considered to be mere diplomatic persiflage, then this might be unimportant. But there is reason to think that the parties to various international Communist agreements have taken the myth of "fraternal relations" seriously and have been genuinely shocked by the outbreak of acrimonious quarrels.

Moreover, the ideological language of Communism is better suited to mortal struggle than constructive discussion. In his younger days, Lenin is said to have been pleased that a colleague said in reference to his debating technique that he had a "deadly bite." From Marx onward this has been the bent of the Communist approach to controversy, and international relations among Communists have been perplexed by reliance on a vocabulary that was designed to devastate one's opponent. This is partly a matter of the tendency to add choice expletives, often drawn from folk-speech, to ideological jargon. Just as Lenin referred to the "deviant" German Marxist Kautsky as "belly-crawling and bootlicking," the Chinese note that Lenin's successors in Moscow have "picked up a stone from a cesspool." It is also a matter of recollecting the tradition of bitter ideological struggle throughout the history of the movement, which lends "revisionist" or "Trotskyist" an intensity that the outsider might underrate.

Finally, the impact of ideological language on Communist approaches to interparty relations is an inhibiting factor. While ideology does not prevent Communist leaders from considering a wide range of tactical expedients in dealing with capitalists, it does inhibit the development of a purely pragmatic policy of national interest, one which would foresee no limits in time or intimacy to friendly relations with "imperialists" states. And while ideology scarcely has prevented the emergence of acute disputes among Communist powers, it inhibits steps that may be taken against antagonistic Communists, as long as they are still defined as such. Here the dogmatic approach to language is especially significant. A party that is *called* Communist is by assumption acceptable as a partner in the long run, while one that has ceased to merit this label deserves only destruction. Life in the world of nuclear weapons and historical complexities not foreseen by the major prophets of Marxism may gradually undermine the inhibitions of ideology, but as long as ideology is reflected in the habitual language of

Communism it will be vitally involved in Communist thought and action.

All of the above suggests that we should not treat the issues among Communist parties and states in separate categories of "ideology," "economics," "military affairs," and so on. Ideology will be involved in any category that we use concerning Communists. This will become clear if we discuss the issues under the headings: territorial issues; economic relations among Communist countries; Communist relations with the non-Communist countries; and domestic policies.*

Territorial Issues

The territorial question may be the most fundamental of all issues in international relations, with explosive potentialities for Communism, but so far its role has been limited in relations between parties and states. The most portentous and most publicized case of a territorial dispute is the Sino-Soviet encounter concerning their long common frontier. This boundary was established in the nineteenth century when the Chinese Empire was unable to defend its territorial integrity against various foreign depredations; and all Chinese nationalist leaders, including Sun Yat-sen, Chiang Kai-shek, and Mao Tse-tung, have held that these injustices should be righted. The most advanced Russian positions in China, Port Arthur, Darien, and the supporting rail lines in Manchuria, which had been lost to Japan in 1905, were regained in 1945. While this could at first be justified to the Chinese Communists as a Soviet check on the "capitalist" China of Chiang Kai-shek, the victory of Mao's forces made the matter a confrontation of national interests. No public argument followed, but the reaffirmation of Soviet rights in Manchuria in treaties signed along with the Sino-Soviet "friendship" pact of February, 1950, must have rankled in Peking. After Stalin was dead and the Chinese Communists had consolidated their power, the Russians were persuaded or obliged to return their imperial holdings in Manchuria in 1955. But this by no means satisfied China. Maps published in Peking as far in advance of the manifest Sino-Soviet split as 1954 showed large areas of the Soviet Union in Asia (adjacent to Central Asia and along the Amur River and Pacific coast), as well as the entire People's Republic of Mongolia, as China *irredenta*. The grievance was made more explicit following the Cuban missile crisis in 1962: Irked by Chinese charges of "capitulation" to imperialism, the Soviets noted that their critics still tolerated such territorial outposts of imperialism as Hong Kong. This barb punctured Chinese reticence on the territorial issue, and in a series of statements they subsequently indicated that the "unequal

* The institutions of international relations among Communists might be treated as an additional issue, but this was discussed in the previous section.

treaties" that had set the existing boundaries should be rectified, that "we have not yet presented our account for this list [of lost territories]." Since then the Soviets have sought to deal with this potential menace by proposing to all heads of state a renunciation of force in settling territorial disputes (December 31, 1963) and by sending a mission to Peking for negotiation of the border question (February 23, 1964). But no progress has been evident, and both sides have claimed provocative acts by the other along the boundary-line.

Eastern Europe, including Russia's western frontier, Germany's eastern frontier, and the frontiers of the smaller countries, is an area of traditionally intense ethnic-territorial disputes, which have been muted since the emergence of a multitude of Communist states there. This relative calm may be better attributed to Soviet hegemony than to a triumph of "fraternal" Communist spirit. One salient feature of this hegemony is the expansion of Soviet frontiers at the end of the Second World War. Particularly important was the annexation of prewar Polish territory and the consequent compensation of Poland at the expense of Germany on the Oder-Neisse line. Since the Western countries, especially the German Federal Republic, have not recognized this settlement, and even Communist East Germany delayed commitment for several years, the Polish Communist regime has felt dependent on Soviet power to maintain its western boundary and dares not hint at the reopening of the question of its Russian frontier. To some extent the same principle applies to Czechoslovakia, which regained territory at the expense of Germany after the war but ceded Carpatho-Ruthenia to the Soviet Union. Without dependence on Soviet insurance of boundaries with the West, conflicting territorial claims are more likely to appear among Communists. Rumania, which after the war regained territory that the Germans had awarded to Hungary (not a very formidable irredentist power today), has not forgotten its old claim to Bessarabia, a province that Russia has annexed several times in the past 150 years. Rumania cannot consider compelling the Soviet Union to hand over this territory, and the unusual conditions that permited Rumania to take Bessarabia in 1918 and 1941 are not likely to recur. Rumanian needling on this matter, however, could have considerable nuisance value and as such could serve as a bargaining counter. The Soviets might be willing to pay off Rumania, possibly through concessions in Comecon, to desist from puncturing the myth that the U.S.S.R. is a voluntary federation of nationalities. In any case the Bessarabian question illustrates the limitations of Soviet hegemony in pacifying old national territorial disputes in Eastern Europe and may presage other disputes in that region.

Some other disputes cropped up in the area soon after the establishment of Communist regimes. The Yugoslav-Albanian frontier cuts through an Albanian-speaking area, which gives the Tirana government a claim against Yugoslavia and Tito's regime a potential claim on all of Albania. The bitterness of this problem is probably fundamental in the Soviet-Albanian dispute, which produced an open split in 1961. During the Second World War, the Yugoslav Communists maintained a patron-client relation with the Albanian partisans, pointing toward the possible absorption of the tiny Communist state by the Yugoslav federation. Each period of Soviet-Yugoslav amity (1945-1948, 1956-1958, 1962-   ) posed for Albania the threat of absorption by the Yugoslavs with the approval of Moscow. Thus the Sino-Albanian alignment since 1961 is potentially a guarantee of Albania's territorial survival. Clearly the "fraternal" spirit of Communism had failed to squelch this ethnic-territorial dispute, which was one of survival for the Albanians. Still worse, the seemingly trivial Balkan squabble played a serious role in aggravating the whole Sino-Soviet dispute.

Communist parties not in power are understandably less directly involved in territorial disputes, since they do not have responsibility for their national borders. To a large extent these parties are engaged only in supporting or not supporting the territorial claims of the "bourgeois" government of their country, more likely the former. Thus Indian Communists back the government of the Congress Party on the Kashmir issue, and the Communists in the Arab states support their governments' claims against Israel. As long as they do not hold power, the Israeli and Arab Communists are not in direct conflict. Sometimes cases arise in which a Communist party not in power finds itself in conflict over territorial questions with a "fraternal" party in power. Such is the case of the Soviet-oriented version of the Indian Communist Party in relation to the Chinese party concerning the disputed Himalayan frontier. Whatever the embarrassment for these Indian Communists in acknowledging that a recently-respected comrade party (that is, the Chinese) could turn imperialistic, it is less painful than insulting aroused Indian nationalism. A somewhat similar case occurred with regard to Yugoslav claims on the area of Trieste and Fiume right after the Second World War. Italian Communists could not be happy about the Slavic-Communist encroachment on "their" territory, but until the Soviet-Yugoslav dispute they were obliged to swallow their true feelings.

The failure of Communists to solve the problem of territorial disputes among themselves is a grave blow to the claim that ideology has solved "the national question." This attractive myth is strikingly represented in doctrinal "classics" by Lenin and Stalin, and the Union of Soviet Socialist Republics is presented as the living embodiment of multinational fraternity.

The slogan of "the right of nations to self-determination," which all Communist parties proclaim, is considered to be the key to the final solution of antagonisms among nations. The argument that this harmonious picture can be maintained in the Soviet Union only through the suppression of political nationalism among the non-Russians seems to be vindicated by the territorial relations between Communist states. But even most critics were formerly willing to grant that voluntary Communist fraternalism seemed to overcome racial antagonisms. In the light of bitter charges that have been raised in the Sino-Soviet dispute even this accomplishment seems denied them. Soviet accusations that the Chinese have used racist arguments among non-Whites when inveighing against the Russians are hard to evaluate with complete accuracy, but the very mention of the issue, despite the inhibitions of earlier Communist propriety, opens a Pandora's Box of racial enmity. How much this issue will inflame territorial disputes among Communists remains to be seen and will probably be influenced by economic considerations, especially the pressures of population on the Chinese economy.

Economic Issues

Economic issues themselves are certainly a major concern in relations among Communists. Although Communists claim to have developed new, harmonious relations of equity and mutual aid in their economic relations, actual experience belies this attractive myth too. The period of the emergence of multiple Communist states provided exceedingly unpromising foundations for equity and fraternity in economic relations. In Europe and Asia the Soviets stripped occupied territory of its industrial equipment and exacted heavy reparations without regard for the interests of probable or possible Communist governments. Following this the Soviets imposed a series of "joint companies" on the new Communist countries, in which the Soviets contributed mainly expropriated "enemy" (Fascist) assets from the country with whom they shared the company. Tito objected to these companies and after Stalin they were acknowledged to have been unfair and were dissolved. Since Stalin, efforts at developing fraternal economic relations have been substantially more genuine, but serious conflicts of interest have arisen all the same.

In large measure all these problems are rooted in the inequalities of wealth that are common to the world at large. In view of the basic idealization of equality of wealth in Marxism, one might expect an international Communist economic system that at least made heroic efforts at eliminating inequities during the transition to the ideal society of abundance and equality. But history and national interest preclude this. Even though it was proclaimed by Soviet authorities in 1959 that all countries would arrive at the final stage of Communist society more or less simultaneously, the Soviet Union would be more than human if it seriously deferred the rewards promised to its own citizens in order to fill China's unavoidably vast needs. It is hard to see how all friction could be avoided on the question of competition between Soviet domestic needs and the Chinese bottomless pit. Considering the long privations endured by China and the severe demands imposed on the Soviet peoples by Stalin and his successors, it would in any case be very hard for both sides to understand fully the feelings of their much richer or poorer neighbor. To a somewhat lesser extent the same could be said of other pairings of Communist countries—Poland and Rumania, for example.

The actual practice of international economic relations among Communists, however, has aggravated this issue far beyond the inevitable minimum. Especially in the Sino-Soviet relationship, the handling of economic aid has suffered from miserliness, tactlessness, and downright betrayal. The miserliness of Soviet assistance to China could be the subject of an extensive book, but it should suffice to note that the Chinese appear to have been obliged to pay for every bit of Soviet aid, including military materiel—much of it obsolescent when sold—which was used in fighting a war in Korea that was originally a Soviet venture. Tactlessness may be illustrated either by the implied Chinese claim that their communes put them ahead of the Soviets in the building of an essentially Communist society or by the extent of Soviet aid to such non-Communist countries as India and Egypt. The equivalent of the Aswan dam would have been most useful to China. The betrayal was notably the Soviet withdrawal of their technicians from China on short notice in 1960, an attempt to extort submission that evidently disturbed even the hardened ex-Stalinist Togliatti.

Economic relations among Communist countries in Europe have been less dramatically beset with tense issues, although the breaking of Soviet and other economic agreements with heretical Yugoslavia in 1948 and Albania in 1961 indicate that harsh pressures are not peculiar to the Sino-Soviet situation within Communism. Comecon has made real strides since 1956 in settling economic issues among a core of Communist states. On the other hand, fraternal spirit was not enough when the majority of the group thought that Rumania should forego her aspirations for industrialization and concentrate on agriculture and the extraction of raw materials. From the Rumanian point of view this was tantamount to insistence that she remain relatively poor in order to enrich her neighbors, and she opted out, much to the detriment of the entire Comecon program.

In relations among non-Communist countries, there has certainly been inequity and even iniquity in the economic relations among them, but it can hardly be said that Communists have brought either improved technique or morality to bear on this problem.

Tactical Issues

The necessity of living in a world that is not wholly Communist presents another thorny issue for the Communists. The myth that there is such a thing as "capitalism" (and its highest stage, "imperialism") is the main cohesive force among Communists. The assumption of "we" (Communists) and "they" (capitalists) runs deep in Communist discussion of international affairs—and they have succeeded in imposing a similar assumption upon most non-Communists. However, the sense of "we" among Communists is far from providing any specific answer to the question of what to do about "them." The mythological premise that "they" are ultimately doomed to destruction provides no clear timetable or explanation of means, and efforts to provide specific policies engender sharp discord among Communists.

Determining the proper degree of hostility and militancy toward the leading "imperialist" countries, notably the United States, presents highly sensitive issues. While some Communist parties, in or out of power, may believe that their interests dictate a tough attitude toward "imperialism," others may see reason to seek relatively harmonious, stabilized relations with "the enemy." Military considerations may play a pre-eminent role in determining the calculation that any given country's Communist leaders make on this matter. The most famous case in point is the Sino-Soviet divergence concerning the United States. The Soviet Union, sharing the monopoly on a complete modern weapons system with the United States, and sharing recognition of the disastrous consequences of using it, has an interest in stable relations with its rival, both to prevent disaster and to preserve its position as one of two dominant powers. China, lacking a similar stake in a world military balance—which relegates her to a secondary position—and professing to see less risk in armed clashes, makes a different, more militant calculation. Is Chinese bluster based on fear of the strenth of an "imperialist" foe who officially aims at supplanting its Communist regime with the one now resident in Taiwan? Or is it based on a belief in the weakness of "paper tigers" that could be routed by a combination of advanced weapons and popular revolution? Perhaps the Chinese themselves are unsure of the answer, but in any case difference in military outlook between Moscow and Peking has produced heated polemics, which have carried over into mutual criticism of the internal character of the two countries. Because she considers the Soviet Union "soft" on American "imperialism," China deems the U.S.S.R. "revisionist" in internal policy. But this superficially consistent argument cannot be taken at its face value. Tito is regarded by the Chinese as an arch-revisionist, a hireling of Wall Street, but at the beginning of the Yugoslav Communist regime it was Tito whose outlook was so hostile toward the West that he urged the Soviets to provide armed support for Yugoslav claims against Italy. Or, one might mention the case of Rumania. Here the Communists were notably antirevisionist in internal policies but supported "peaceful coexistence" with the West with a sincerity that need not be doubted, owing to Rumania's self-interest in expanded economic relations with the European capitalist countries.

Quite a different kind of military consideration encourages conflicting Communist perspectives on internal revolutions and the proper posture of parties that would like to come to power. Communists in such countries as South Vietnam and Columbia, encouraged by leading Communist parties, believe that armed seizure of power through guerilla action is both feasible and worth the cost. On the other side, leading Communists in Italy, France, and India see no hope in violence, but some real possibilities in parliamentary campaigning. While it is possible to attempt to develop a flexible program that permits each national Communist party to devise its own tactics, militant or peaceful, it has proven difficult to obtain sincere cohesion between such diverse types as the parliamentarian and the guerilla. While both may agree that American "imperialism" is a "Bad Thing," there is usually quite a difference in the emphasis that each would place on this. The guerilla wants to whip up a frenzy of hate, while the parliamentarian wants to assure uncommitted voters that he is not the extremist that his rivals accuse him of being. The guerilla, perceiving current politics as a tense military battle, is likely to support some form of centralized international Communist leadership, while the parliamentarian, hoping to escape from accusations of subservience to Russia (or possibly China), is inclined toward "polycentrism," a euphemism for national autonomy.

The confusion concerning the posture of parties not in power toward the capitalists has been further increased by the Sino-Soviet quarrel. While the Chinese Communists profess to reject "revisionism" in Italy, they supported the policy of the Indonesian Communists before the abortive *coup* there in 1965, even though Indonesian Communists were following a policy of peaceful maneuver and support of the non-Communist Sukarno. The basic issue appears not to have been correct policy toward the seizure of power, but correct policy in the Sino-Soviet dispute The Italians were guilty of supporting Russia and even Yugoslavia, while the Indonesians were behind China. It is always easy for one Communist to find fault with another's tactics, if he is free to do so, and the issue of policy toward capitalism can serve as a handy stick with which to beat an adversary.

Still another dimension of this issue appears in the former colonial or semicolonial countries that in recent years have produced strong nationalist movements. The classical Leninist doctrine is to treat all such movements as temporary allies against "imperialism," despite the fact that such regimes are basically not Communist. The practical interpretation of this doctrine, however, opens additional opportunities for argument. In his later years Stalin, recollecting his unfortunate experience with the Kuomingtang in the 1920's, maintained a suspicious attitude toward such nationalist movements, but by 1955 his successors had taken a demonstrative trip to Burma and India, and the Chinese had sent a delegation to the Bandung conference of Afro-Asian leaders. From this point forward the very opportunities for Communist maneuver among the new nationalist regimes and parties has provided fuel for discord. One difficulty is most strikingly illustrated by the case of India, which was for a time treated amicably by both Moscow and Peking. By 1959, however, the clash of interests between China and India in the Himalayas posed the Soviets with the choice of abandoning India as a valued, neutralist friend or of incurring Chinese wrath. The Soviets, who probably were not consulted by the Chinese when the latter adopted their hard line against India, considered that they had every right to continue the policy of amity toward India, in which they had a considerable political and economic stake. As a result, Soviet-built jets, flown by Chinese and by Indians, came to confront each other across the Himalayas.

Another type of difficulty is the one formerly experienced in China, when the native Communists were obliged to accede to Soviet support for the anti-Communist nationalist movement in the country. In recent years the case of Egypt illustrates the problem well. The Soviet Union has sent substantial economic and political support to Nasser, an active "anti-imperialist," even though he persecuted the Communists in his own country. These unfortunates presumably were expected to understand that the higher interest of the revolution is represented by the policy of the Soviet Union and its close allies (and also by Nasser's friend Tito). The best that can be said of the solution of this conflict of interests among Communists is that the victimized ones, such as the Egyptians, are usually too feeble to afford a protest. But, like Mao, they may have the opportunity some day to repay the callousness of their senior comrades.

Finally, there are revolutionary nationalist movements whose leaders are not avowedly full-fledged Communists, but come close enough to it to tempt leading Communist parties to treat them not only as allies against "imperialism," but also as comrades at the edge of the Communist movement. Examples include Touré's regime in Guinea, Keita's in Mali, and—while they lasted—Sukarno's in Indonesia, Ben Bella's in Algeria and Nkrumah's in Ghana. In each of these cases native Communists have supported the regime, which in turn was considered a "national democracy"—a quasi-Communist government in the process of becoming a full-fledged one. This, however, raised the question of the definition of Communism precisely at a time when the two most powerful parties were engaged in ferocious quarrels over just this issue. Will a given "national democracy" become Muscovite or Pekinese Communists? Who determines when and how such a movement has qualified for membership in the Communist community with a legitimate voice in any conferences that may be held? Uncertainty on these points has provided a fresh field for Sino-Soviet rivalry and provoked these powers to engage in competitive persuasion among the national democracies. Even smaller Communist parties, notably the Yugoslav and Italian, have taken fairly independent positions as mentors of African nationalist-revolutionaries.

Domestic Policies

After some other source of contention has developed, almost any domestic policy of one Communist country may serve as an issue in its relations with another. Whether the specific domestic matter is great or small, it may be treated as a sign of portentous ideological error. For example, the great Chinese program of communes as a short-cut to the ultimate Communist society as well as the relatively minor matter of the execution by the Albanians of a few party members were both treated by Khrushchev as signs of bourgeois nationalism. In the course of the Soviet press campaign against China in 1964 even the Chinese rejection of their traditional cuisine was the subject of extended comment.

It may seem hard to reconcile the alleged principle of noninterference in the internal affairs of another party with such concern for the domestic policies of one's fraternal comrades abroad. But the very idea of fraternity implies a basis for concern with domestic affairs. And it is often true that the domestic policies of one country have direct bearing on the interests of another. The Chinese commune campaign and the later "cultural revolution" implied a claim to ideological superiority over the Soviet and other Communists. Or, the Soviet demolition of the Stalin cult was a blow to the prestige of foreign Communists who had supported it, just as the abrupt removal of Khrushchev was somewhat humiliating to leaders abroad who had identified their careers with his.

In Stalin's day it seems to have been understood that the Soviet Union had a legitimate interest in almost any aspect of the domestic policies of East European Communist countries, while these countries were not to have any opinion except adulation concerning Soviet domestic affairs. In his letters to Tito Stalin made an issue variously of individual personnel of the Yugoslav foreign ministry, Yugoslav agrarian policy, and procedural arrangements within the Yugoslav party. In later years the Soviet Union has not been in a position to express itself so freely on the domestic policies of other Communist countries, while the latter have increasingly commented critically on Soviet home affairs, including even such details as the Soviet persecution in 1966 of a pair of nonconformist writers.

In general, Communist leaders probably realize that their relations with one another will be smoother if they minimize concern for one another's domestic policies. But their common commitment to ideological "correctness" makes it difficult for them to overlook those domestic policies of their cohorts that reveal some tendency to "deviation."

In sum, the Communists have not succeeded in laying to rest most of the familiar issues that produce conflict in international affairs, and, by the very nature of their ideology, find themselves faced with additional perplexities.

THE DOCUMENTARY EVIDENCE

Some time in the future, perhaps far in the future, there will be much more complete evidence concerning international relations among Communists than is now available. Memoirs, secret protocols of treaties, policy papers designed for internal consumption, more or less complete international correspondence, and many other documents may illuminate the study of international relations among Communists in the middle of the twentieth century as comparable documents have illuminated the diplomacy of the nineteenth century. Such a level of research cannot now be attained concerning our topic, but for the reader who prefers not to wait indefinitely there is already an important body of reliable evidence. Before passing on to selections from the documents themselves it is desirable to survey the general character of the evidence and the problems of understanding that it presents.

Unilateral Documents

First, there are unilateral documents, emanating from a single Communist party or state. Many of the important documents of this type are party resolutions or similar formal statements of policy—for example, the 1958 program of the Yugoslav Communists or the 1964 resolution of the Rumanian party. The character of Communism lends such documents an especially authoritative flavor. They are not only major policy statements but purportedly emanations of the supreme Marxist wisdom that each party claims to monopolize within its country. When the congress or central committee of a given party formally announces its policy on relations with other Communist parties or states it is exercising, or pretending to exercise, its sovereignty as a party, and it does not require the ratification of its government (if it controls one) or the consent of other Communist parties. By the same token, unilateral party resolutions and the like do not represent an international transaction and do not have any necessary effect upon foreign parties (the Chinese rebuked the Soviets for treating decisions of their 1956 party congress as if they *were* internationally binding). But they are necessary, more so than similar documents in conventional diplomacy, because they represent the ideological pretension of infallibility that is basic to Communism.

Communist states also issue unilateral declarations that bear on relations among Communists, especially when pronouncements deal with such matters as military forces, which are formally the concern of the state rather than the party. Examples in this collection are the Soviet declaration issued during the Eastern European crisis of 1956 and the Soviet and Chinese statements of 1963 concerning the nuclear test ban treaty. These are likely to have more specific or technical content than party declarations, but lack the broad, ideological significance of party resolutions. In view of the control of every Communist state by the party, it would be futile to attempt to discriminate between the level of authority of party and state declarations.

Only slightly less weighty than these declarations are speeches by party leaders which represent unilateral policy declarations, such as Togliatti's discussion of "polycentrism" in his speech to the June, 1956, meeting of the central committee of the Italian Communist Party, or Khrushchev's attack on Albania in his concluding address to the twenty-second congress of his party. Although such oral pronouncements may be closely related to some formal party resolution, they may also stand by themselves as serious but less fully committed statements of policy. In both of the examples cited, major speeches before party gatherings were new excursions upon sensitive subjects, and the speaker probably wanted more flexibility to negotiate or retreat than would have been convenient if the gist of his argument had been embodied in a formal resolution. In at least some cases the edge of the speaker's thought may be less blunted—by consultation with influential associates —than in other cases, although it is sometimes true that modifications of especially sharp statements occur through editorial changes that are made when the speech is published. Some speeches are delivered to closed meetings and then withheld from publication, unlike resolutions and programs, which are almost always published in the party press. Such confidential speeches almost always remain unknown to the outside world, which for our study is especially regrettable in view of the probability that the Communist leaders speak most frankly within the closed circle of their own party's elite. It is hard to say how frequently such speeches are revealed to Communist parties of other countries. Khrushchev's "secret" speech of February, 1956, attacking Stalin is said to have been released in confidential copies to some non-Soviet Communists, but this remains an isolated instance, and not a very encouraging one with regard to security in view of the subsequent leak to the Americans.

Still less committal than major speeches are articles in official party publications, especially newspapers. Considering that these organs are carefully controlled by the supreme Communist authorities in each country and that their editors would not think of taking the initiative in expressing opinions on international relations among Communists, such articles should not be taken lightly. Articles in the official party press are understood to be the voice of the whole party and can serve as a convenient form of communication to all foreign parties, an efficient substitute for letters, and a more flexible medium of expression than resolutions. In the period of Soviet supremacy over a large number of Communist parties, articles in the Soviet press certainly served as a series of "orders of the day" on matters of general concern, such as reaction to the Marshall Plan. Later, as the Sino-Soviet quarrel emerged, newspaper articles served as a kind of "open letter without an addressee"—that is, the addressee, or object of attack, could be determined by an informed reader, despite the absence of explicit identification in the article. A distinguished case in point was the article, "Long Live Leninism!," published in the Chinese press in April, 1960, which opened their critique of Soviet policy without specifically saying so. Had this approach not led in time to more direct vituperation, one might consider it fairly tactful, allowing the addressee of the criticism to mend his ways with minimum embarrassment. Still later in the qaurrel the two main parties were scarcely on speaking terms, having carried unpleasant correspondence to the point at which more correspondence seemed futile and perhaps self-demeaning. In this situation the medium of newspaper articles again came into its own, serving as a substitute for conversation or correspondence with an odious adversary. This was noticeable after one increasingly heated round of Sino-Soviet correspondence that concluded in July, 1963, and again after a second in 1964.

When newspaper articles convey preliminary, subtle disagreement between Communist parties, they may involve the Marxist circumlocution that Western commentators have sometimes called "esoteric communication." In this usage one meets not only the usual problems of understanding Marxist terminology but also those of decoding expression that is meant to say more than it means literally. For example, at the beginning of the 1960s, the Chinese newspapers had not arrived at overt castigation of the Soviet leaders and referred to "some comrades," or for a time the Soviet press referred to Albania when it meant China, while the Chinese substituted "Yugoslavia" for "Soviet Union." The parties of secondary or lower importance have often tried to maintain a position of qualified support for one or another of the major antagonists within Communism by using circumlocutions, or tactful omission of this or that point, to state their positions. For the detailed study of international relations among Communists, especially in certain periods, expertise in "esoteric communication" is important, but in our present introduction, which relies mostly on documents that are fairly explicit, this special art is of marginal significance.* (The present anthology, incidentally, includes few articles from Communist periodicals because space requirements dictate the selection only of those documents that reveal Communist policy in its more authoritative, full-developed forms.)

Multilateral Documents

Closely related to the unilateral category of documents are the letters that constitute bilateral correspondence between Communist parties. Such letters originate with a single party but are fully intelligible only as part of a multilateral context, for they either constitute or invite replies. Some of the letters that we have were originally intended to remain confidential but became public as a result of interparty quarrels. The Soviets made the first leak as part of their campaign against Tito, circulating copies of their letters to the heretical party more or less publicly in Yugoslavia during 1948. Tito retaliated, perhaps to Stalin's surprise, by making fully public release of both sides in the correspondence. Somewhat similar circumstances motivated Chinese release of some of the Sino-Soviet correspondence in 1963-1964, although in this episode the likelihood of a breach of confidence must have been pretty clear from the beginning. On occasion during the Sino-Soviet exchange a party has published a letter dispatched to its adversary almost immediately, making it in effect an open letter or purely propagandistic document. This practice, which is intentionally rude to the addressee and forestalls him from publishing the letter first, was followed by the Chinese in their letter of June 14, 1963. Some other, relatively less important, correspondence between parties is published soon after composition for the opposite reason—as a gesture of friendship. This is true of letters of greet-

---

* A good discussion of esoteric communication in Communist international relations appears in a volume that provides a lot of material to be read with this problem in mind: Alexander Dallin (ed.), *Diversity in International Communism: A Documentary Record, 1961-1963* (New York: Columbia University Press, 1963), introtion, pp. xxxvii-vliv, by Dallin and Zbigniew Brzezinski. See also Donald S. Zagoria, *The Sino-Soviet Dispute, 1956-1961* (Princeton: Princeton University Press, 1962), "A Note on Methodology," pp. 24-35.

ing from one party to another, congratulations on the anniversary of a national-Communist holiday, and the like, such as the greeting of the Chinese party to the twenty-second congress of the Soviet party. While these tend to be deceptively bland and fraternal, they are sometimes important for the esoteric communication they contain through emphasis or deemphasis of various issues or through warmth or lack of it.

We know that some interparty correspondence exists but remains confidential. This seems to be especially true of major circular letters—identical letters sent to a number of parties. Despite the fact that a considerable number of parties receives them, it appears that a serious inhibition concerning the publication of these documents has existed, in contrast with the attitude toward more strictly bilateral letters. There is definite evidence that there have been circular letters from the Soviet party in September, 1956 (warning against Yugoslav influence), in June, 1960 (in connection with the Bucharest conference), from the Chinese party in September, 1960, and from the Soviet party in November, 1960 (both in connection with the Moscow conference of 81 parties), from the Soviet party in February, 1964 (pointing toward an anti-Chinese conference), again from them in early 1966, and from the Polish party in 1966 (Soviet-inspired, in connection with the twenty-third congress of the Soviet party). Through allusions in published letters, we also know of a bilateral exchange between the Soviet and Chinese parties in 1962 (Soviet letters dated February 22 and May 31; a Chinese letter dated April 7), and Soviet-Albanian letters which have remained confidential. It is conceivable that much more interparty correspondence exists than we know anything about. Despite the repeated indiscretions that have provided the outsider with interparty correspondence, the relations between most Communist parties most of the time are so secretive and disciplined that it is possible for a large volume of exchanges to occur without public leaks occurring. On the other hand, the impression remains that bilateral interparty relations are weakly developed, lacking an established institutional system of personal representation, as noted earlier. Quite likely correspondence between parties (in the name of their respective central committees) is regarded as an exceptional activity, an exercise of lofty ideological authority that should be used only when exceptional problems exist. If this is true, then the non-Communist student already may have at his disposal a substantial part of the post-Comintern correspondence between Communist parties, despite the unavailability of most of the circular letters noted. Because the interparty correspondence that has been published is a highly authoritative medium of expression dealing with vital issues, it has been used extensively in this anthology.

When Communist parties or states conduct multilateral negotiations, communiqués or treaties may result. Party and state bodies alike may issue communiqués on meetings, but only states sign treaties. This signifies that treaties deal with matters such as trade or military affairs that are formally the concern of the state. These can be important questions in their own right, but they do not determine the fundamental issues between Communist countries, questions of general concurrence or hostility. Such basic questions are always presented in the ideological language of Communism, while treaties between Communist states are strictly nonideological in form, using the language of conventional diplomacy. Thus the Sino-Soviet treaty of 1950 might just as well have been between the U.S.S.R. and a non-Communist country, for all it says. This is also true of the important multilateral Warsaw Treaty. One cannot exclude the possibility that these treaties or others between Communist states include secret protocols of great importance, as did the Nazi-Soviet pact of 1939, but so far no specific evidence on such additional instruments has appeared. What may be most significant about the Sino-Soviet treaty with respect to specifically Communist issues is that there was in 1950 no parallel joint-party communiqué. Such bilateral and multilateral joint statements are common enough. They serve in place of treaties in interparty relations and they may attempt to commit their signatories to some common point of view, which may imply joint action.

In any case, multilateral declarations or statements of a number of Communist parties constitute the most authoritative documentary instrument in international relations among Communists. The "Declaration" of the twelve-party conference of 1957 and the "Statement" of the eighty-one party conference of 1960 (there is no apparent reason for the distinction in their labels) are officially regarded as the quintessence of ideological insight and as binding super-treaties among parties. Precisely because of this reverent attitude toward these documents, they must be read with caution. The ostensible consensus on which these documents rest their claim to importance was achieved by platitudinous phrases and compromise. In studying a treaty one much watch for legalistic detail, but in analyzing Communist international party agreements one must try to fathom the fundamental antagonisms beneath the surface of unanimity. Here a knowledge of Communist ideological language and the specific historical context of a given document is the basis for insight.

No other multiparty statements can equal the pretensions of those of 1957 and 1960. The resolutions of the Cominform were more limited in origin and scope, while the communiqué of the March, 1965, "consultative meeting" reflected in its vacuity the deadlock in the Sino-Soviet dispute. Lack of substance has also characterized most communiqués of the fairly frequent bilateral meetings between parties, but more as a matter of security than as a reflection of failure to decide anything. The communiqué of the Soviet-Polish meeting of November, 1956 (technically a party-state meeting, because some specifically state matters, such as troops, were involved), shows that agreements of considerable importance may be reached in bilateral party meetings. The results, however, are usually concealed behind an empty statement about "discussions in a friendly atmosphere." The numerous examples of this type of document would serve no purpose in this anthology.

In sum, the documentary evidence on international relations among Communists is uneven and incomplete, but sometimes acutely revealing and in general adequate to provide an introduction to the subject. While an elementary acquaintance with Marxism-Leninism is useful, the same kind of critical judgment and imagination that is needed to study international affairs in general is the main prerequisite for a rewarding reading of the documents that follow. They are basically arranged in chronological order, with deviations from this insofar as necessary to keep closely related documents together. Many of the documents appear with substantial excisions by the editor, partly to make it possible to include a wide variety of materials and partly because of the stupefying redundancy in many Communist documents. While long discussions of the context of each document could be provided, the editor believes that they can speak for themselves quite eloquently with only a skeletal commentary. This framework does not pretend to constitute a general narrative of the subject. Although there is a large literature on various aspects of international relations among Communists, the study of the subject as a whole is in its infancy, and it is doubtful that it is now possible to provide a good general treatment of it from the viewpoint of either political science or history. Until it becomes possible to write such books, the best introduction to this new branch of international relations remains the basic though incomplete, evidence that follows.

I

STALINISM

AND THE FAÇADE

OF UNITY, 1943-1953

Compared to subsequent years, the last decade of Stalin's reign seems to have been one of unity and stability among Communists. There was a real basis for this appearance. The predominant position of the Soviet Union among the Communists of the world was strengthened as the tide of war turned in its favor. The dissolution of the Comintern at about this time was an act of the Soviet leadership, probably designed to simplify control over foreign Communists, rather than a secessionist rebellion on the part of the latter. As the Red Army moved across Eastern Europe and as German and Japanese hegemony in Europe and Asia collapsed, the development of a Soviet-centered Communist system emerged. No power was able or willing to block the process by which Soviet military occupation and political influence converted Eastern European countries into Communist states, and until 1948 the avowedly Stalinist leaders of these states and the strong Communist parties in such countries as France and Italy seemed securely in line behind the Kremlin leadership. In Soviet alignment at the U.N.; in their rejection of Marshall Plan aid; in their cultural isolation from the West and Russification; in their new, Soviet-style constitutions; in all these the new Communist states appeared to be part of a disciplined empire that might well extend to the Atlantic in the absence of strong American resistance in Europe. The very exception to the rule, the heresy of Tito's Yugoslavia in 1948, seemed to lead to a reinforcement of Soviet predominance through the purging, often accompanied by torture and executions, of Eastern European Communists who were considered to be too concerned with the interests of their particular nations. After June, 1948, the Cominform organ, *For a Lasting Peace, For a People's Democracy!,* served as a clearing house of abuse for Tito and his "imperialist masters." The outbreak of the Korean war provided a fresh focus for effusions of solidarity, actively involving the new Chinese Communist state after it entered the war in October, 1950. To the outside world there seemed to be very effective harmony between the Soviet-supported North Korean Communist regime and the Peking regime, with which Stalin had concluded a treaty of friendship in 1950. Perhaps the most striking symbols of the apparent unity of all Communists in this period were the hysterical accusations of biological warfare against United States forces under U.N. command in Korea and the concurrent peace movement, in which Communist participants from many lands exuded fraternal spirit.

Over the entire, seemingly monolithic "camp" (*lager* in Russian, a deliberate choice of the military term) loomed the image of Stalin. Although formally the leader of only one party, he was accorded a semideified status in all Communist parties (except in Yugoslavia after 1948), and was in symbol the supreme international commander. No doubt there was real authority behind this prestige, for he carried on the personal direction of many alien Communist parties when he wished to and controlled the Soviet party apparatus that gave orders to most other Communist parties. With only a little exaggeration one might describe the postwar "camp" of Communism as an essentially feudal form, that is, the organization of political power on the basis of fealty to a personal overlord, who returns the favor by acknowledging the authority of each vassal over a particular fief.

Stalin no doubt intended that onlookers should be impressed by the imposing façade of unity and solidarity of his international order. Quite likely he also meant for this display to distract attention from the uncertainties and weaknesses that lay within the order and its master. The last decade of Stalin's life was a time of exceptional change in world affairs as a whole, and it was no simple task to adjust international relations within Communism to the new and uncertain environment. The documents that follow display various symptoms of uncertainty and vacillation. The announcements concerning the dissolution of the Comintern and the establishment of the Cominform (Documents 1-3) should be compared in their attitude toward international Communist organization. Zhdanov, one of Stalin's senior lieutenants and the specialist in international Communism, told the founding conference of the Cominform that "some comrades" had misread the meaning of the announcement of dissolution with respect to formal international organization. But the literal meaning of the resolution on dissolution did in fact suggest that Stalin had doubts about formal organization, and the limited, flimsy structure of the Cominform suggests that he still had not made up his mind on this matter. The Sino-Soviet Treaty of 1950 (Document 9) reenforces this impression, considering its reserved, limited character and the absence of any declared, formal interparty ties between the two fore-most Communist regimes.

If Stalin was uncertain what to do about world-wide international relations among Communists, he seems to have been equally uncertain about the forms of organization that might be developed within the limited sphere of Eastern Europe. One indication of this mood was the prevalence of the "front" of Communists and other left-wing parties as the chief vehicle for the promotion of Soviet interests within the countries that became satellites. Lenin had rejected coalition with other left-wing parties in Russia, but Stalin, despite his military power, seems to have preferred coalition "fronts" for their flexibility in the Eastern European situation. As the case of the "People's Front" in Yugoslavia had demonstrated even before the end of the war, this political form could be a mere disguise for full Communist authority, but it could also serve as a transitional instrument of maneuver, leading more or less rapidly toward a Communist regime according to the internal conditions in a given country and the posture of the Western powers. Stalin was probably unsure at the end of the war what the non-Communist great powers, the possessors of a monopoly on atomic weapons, would do about Communist take-overs, especially if clever and determined local resistance made the process excessively brutal. The front of left-wing parties could be used for accelerated Communization if conditions seemed ripe or for maintaining a more limited degree of Communist influence in strategic areas if the risks of acceleration seemed too great. In actuality the weakness of the West and of Eastern European anti-Communists made it possible to convert all the fronts into definitely Communist organizations by 1948. An analogous flexibility may be seen in the Communist presentation of the "People's Democracies," which the fronts promoted as the new state-form. At first this supposedly new type of government was officially described as an alternative to either a "bourgeois democracy" or a Communist "dictatorship of the proletariat," but by 1947 it was deemed safe to acknowledge that the "people's democracy" was a "dictatorship of the proletariat without the Soviet form." Considering the annexation of the Baltic states, it seemed possible for a time that the forms of progressive Communization might lead to the inclusion of the "people's democracies" in the Soviet federal state. According to one letter published by the Yugoslav Communists, one of their own leaders, Kardelj, in June, 1945, told the Soviet ambassador that he hoped for such an outcome. The reply, in a version presumably approved by Stalin in 1948, did not exclude this eventuality, even though it referred to Yugoslavia as an independent state at the time of the conversation.

An alternative possibility (or conceivably a transitional stage on the path to inclusion in the U.S.S.R.) that was discussed with Stalin's assent was a federation within Eastern Central Europe. Tito and the Bulgarian leader Dimitrov were the main proponents of this approach, which evidently started with Yugoslav-Bulgarian federation and aimed at a general Eastern-European Communist federation. A bilateral treaty signed in August, 1947, pointed the way toward this goal, but in January, 1948, the Soviet organ *Pravda* abruptly dismissed any federalist planning in East Europe, quite possibly because Stalin had decided that Tito was excessively ambitious and independent.

Having obliged the Yugoslav Communist state to continue its separate integrity, Stalin soon found that this provided new difficulties, in particular the problem of dealing with a genuinely independent—even obstreperous—Communist regime. The published record of the confrontation of the Soviet Union and Yugoslavia in 1948 and 1949 (Documents 4-8) reveals an escalation of Soviet chastisements that are harsh and mendacious, but does not reflect any established policy for dealing with deviant satellites. The situation was a new one and Stalin was not sure what to do. The range of alternative presumably ran from verbal reproof to invasion, and Stalin in the course of two years moved up the scale to the edge of full-scale military action, at which point he stopped, baffled. It seems that he was deterred much less by the armed strength of isolated Yugoslavia than by uncertainty concerning the internal repercussions of such an act among other Communist parties. His mistrust of the member parties of the Cominform is well illustrated by his unwillingness to bring the matter to a Cominform meeting *before* the split was an accomplished fact. The subsequent purging of leading Eastern European Communists on charges of Titoist treason, beginning in Hungary in September, 1949, was a show of ruthlessness based on insecurity and uncertainty rather than any positive program for Communist international relations.

By the end of Stalin's life, international relations among Communists seemed to have become somewhat stabilized, just as the conflict between Communism and the outside world seemed to have settled down on relatively clear lines. Tito was in limbo but clearly surviving. The other Communist states of Eastern Europe appeared well-established and definitely subordinated to Stalin on a bilateral basis. The Chinese and Soviet Communists were seemingly settled on a course of very restrained fraternity, in which Stalin did not press for the kind of authority he had exercised in Europe and most other areas, while Mao respected Soviet seniority and did not importune unduly for economic or military support. The nonruling parties had lost hope of immediate revolution almost everywhere. The Cominform had lapsed into a mere guise for a Soviet-run newspaper, and no further efforts at international organization were afoot.

But not only the symbolism of solidarity but also much of the real coherence among Communists at the opening of 1953 depended on Stalin personally. The parallel with feudal politics suggests the potential difficulty of dynastic succession. Too much depended on one man and too little had been developed in the way of international organization and practice among Communists. Moreover, the degree of success that Stalin had achieved in holding things together was to a considerable measure based on the wanton exploitation of loyalty and on extortion that had laid up a store of resentment.

The Dissolution
of the Comintern

DOCUMENT 1

"Resolution of the Presidium of the Executive Committee of the Communist International," May 15, 1943.

THE HISTORIC ROLE of the Communist International, which was formed in 1919 as a result of the political collapse of the overwhelming majority of the old prewar workers' parties, consisted in defending the teachings of Marxism from vulgarization and distortion by the opportunist elements of the workers' movement, in assisting the consolidation in a number of countries of the vanguard of the advanced workers into a genuine workers' party, in helping them to mobilize the masses of workers for the defense of their economic and political interests, for the struggle against fascism and the war for which it was preparing, for the defense of the Soviet Union, as the main bulwark against fascism. The Communist International at the same

From *Bol'shevik*, no. 10, 1943. Editor's translation.

time exposed the real meaning of the "Anti-Communist Pact" [between Germany, Italy and Japan—ED.] as an instrument in the preparation by Hitler of the war. It ceaselessly exposed, long before the war, the vicious subversive work of the Hitlerites in foreign states, who disguised it by screaming about the so-called interference of the Communist International in the internal affairs of these states.

But long before the war it became more and more clear that, as a result of complications in both the internal and international circumstances of individual countries, the solution of problems of the workers' movements of individual countries on the strength of any sort of international center would meet insuperable obstacles.

The profound distinctions of the different historical paths of development of the separate countries of the world and even the contradictions in their social orders, differences in the level and tempo of their social and political development, and finally, differences in the consciousness and organization of the workers conditioned the various tasks that stand before the working class of separate countries.

The whole course of events in the past quarter of a century and the experience accumulated by the Communist International convincingly showed that the organizational form of uniting workers, chosen by the First Congress of the Communist International, which answered the demands of the first period of the growth of the workers' movement, has been ever more outgrown by the growth of this movement and the complication of its tasks in separate countries and has even become a drag on the further strengthening of the national workers' parties.

The world war that the Hitlerites have unleashed has still further sharpened the differences in the situation of the separate countries, marking out a profound dividing line between the countries that have fallen under Hitlerite tyranny and the freedom-loving countries that are united in a powerful anti-Hitler coalition. . . .

Guided by the teachings of the founders of Marxism-Leninism, Communists have never been advocates of the preservation of organizational forms that have outlived themselves. They have always subordinated the forms of organization of the workers' movement and the methods of work of this organization to the basic political interests of the workers' movement as a whole, to the peculiarities of given concrete historical circumstances, and to those tasks that follow directly from these circumstances. They remember the example of the great Marx, who united the foremost workers in the ranks of the Working Men's International Association, and after the First International had fulfilled its historical task of laying the foundations for the development of workers' parties in the countries of Europe and America, carried out, as a result of the fruition of the demands for the creation of mass national workers' parties, the dissolution of the First International inasmuch as this form of organization already did not correspond to these demands.

In consideration of the above factors and taking into account the growth and political maturity of the Communist parties and their leading cadres in the separate countries, and also having in view the fact that during the present war a series of sections [of the Comintern—ED.] have raised the question of the dissolution of the Communist International as the leading center of the international workers' movement, the Presidium of the Executive Committee of the Communist International, not having the possibility in the conditions of the world war to convene a Congress of the Communist International, ventures to submit for ratification to the sections of the Communist International the following proposal:

> To disband the Communist International as the leading center of the international workers' movement, freeing the sections of the Communist International from the obligations stemming from the statutes and decisions of the Congresses of the Communist International.

The Presidium of the Executive of the Communist International calls on all adherents of the Communist International to concentrate their strength on the world-wide support and active participation in the war of liberation of the peoples and states of the anti-Hitler coalition for the speediest defeat of the mortal enemy of the workers—German fascism and its allies and vassals.

Members of the Presidium of the Executive Committee
of the Communist International:
Gottwald, Dimitrov, Zhdanov, Kolarov, Koplenig,
Kuusinen, Manuilsky, Marti, Pieck, Thorez, Florin, Ercoli.*

* Ercoli became better known after the war as Togliatti. Gottwald (Czech), Dimitrov (Bulgarian), Kolarov (Bulgarian), and Pieck (German) played leading roles in the postwar satellite governments of their respective countries, while Marti and Thorez (French) and Ercoli (Italian) served as apparently obedient Stalinists, leading parties that belonged to the Cominform—ED.

The Formation
of the Cominform

DOCUMENT 2

Announcement of Establishment of the
Cominform, November, 1947.

THE REPRESENTATIVES OF the Communist Party of Yugoslavia, the Bulgarian Workers' Party (Communists), the Communist Party of Rumania, the Hungarian Communist Party, the Polish Workers' Party, the Communist Party of the Soviet Union (Bolsheviks), the Communist Party of France, the Communist Party of Czechosolovakia, and the Communist Party of Italy, having exchanged views on the international situation, have agreed upon the following declaration.

Fundamental changes have taken place in the international situation as a result of the Second World War and in the postwar period.

These changes are characterized by a new disposition of the basic political forces operating on the world arena, by a change in the relations among the victor states in the Second World War, and their realignment.

While the war was on, the Allied States in the war against Germany and Japan went together and comprised one camp. However, already during the war there were differences in the Allied camp as regards the definition of both war aims and the tasks of the postwar peace settlement. The Soviet Union and the other democratic countries regarded as their basic war aims the restoration and consolidation of democratic order in Europe, the eradication of fascism and the prevention of the possibility of new aggression on the part of Germany, and the establishment of a lasting all-round cooperation among the nations of Europe. The United States of America, and Britain in agreement with them, set themselves another aim in the war: to rid themselves of competitors on the market (Germany and Japan) and to establish their dominant position. This difference in the definition of war aims and the tasks of the postwar settlement grew more profound after the war. Two diametrically opposed political lines took shape: on the one side

From *For a Lasting Peace, For a People's Democracy!*, November 10, 1947.

the policy of the U.S.S.R. and the other democratic countries directed at undermining imperialism and consolidating democracy, and on the other side, the policy of the United States and Britain directed at strengthening imperialism and stifling democracy. Inasmuch as the U.S.S.R. and the countries of the new democracy became obstacles to the realization of the imperialist plans of struggle for world domination and smashing of democratic movements, a crusade was proclaimed against the U.S.S.R. and the countries of the new democracy, bolstered also by threats of a new war on the part of the most zealous imperialist politicians in the United States of America and Britain. . . .

The principal danger for the working class today lies in underestimating their own strength and overestimating the strength of the imperialist camp. Just as the Munich policy untied the hands of Hitlerite aggression in the past, so yielding to the new line in the policy of the United States and that of the imperialist camp is bound to make its inspirers still more arrogant and aggressive. Therefore, the Communist Parties must take the lead in resisting the plans of imperialist expansion and aggression in all spheres— state, political, economic, and ideological; they must close their ranks, unite their efforts on the basis of a common anti-imperialist and democratic platform, and rally around themselves all the democratic and patriotic forces of the nation.

Resolution on Interchange of Experience and Coordination of Activities of the Parties Represented at the Conference

The Conference states that the absence of contacts among the Communist Parties participating at this Conference is a serious shortcoming in the present situation. Experience has shown that such lack of contacts among the Communist Parties is wrong and harmful. The need for interchange of experience and voluntary coordination of action of the various Parties is particularly keenly felt at the present time in view of the growing complication of the postwar international situation, a situation in which the lack of connections among the Communist Parties may prove detrimental to the working class.

In view of this, the participants in the Conference have agreed on the following:

1. To set up an Information Bureau consisting of representatives of the Communist Party of Yugoslavia, the Bulgarian Workers' Party (Communists), the Communist Party of Rumania, the Hungarian Communist Party, the Polish Workers' Party, the Communist Party of the Soviet Union (Bol-

sheviks), the Communist Party of France, the Communist Party of Czecho-slovakia, and the Communist Party of Italy.

2. To charge the Information Bureau with the organization of inter-change of experience, and if need be, coordination of the activities of the Communist Parties on the basis of mutual agreement.

3. The Information Bureau is to consist of two representatives from each Central Committee, the delegations of the Central Committees to be appointed and replaced by the Central Committees.

4. The Information Bureau is to have a printed organ—a fortnightly and subsequently, a weekly. The organ is to be published in French and Russian, and when possible, in other languages as well.

5. The Information Bureau is to be located in the city of Belgrade.

DOCUMENT 3

Speech by A. A. Zhdanov to the Founding Conference of the Cominform, November, 1947.

. . . THE DISSOLUTION OF the Comintern, which conformed to the demands of the development of the labor movement in the new historical situation, played a positive role. The dissolution of the Comintern once and for all disposed of the slanderous allegation of the enemies of Communism and the labor movement that Moscow was interfering in the internal affairs of other states, and that the Communist Parties in the various countries were acting not in the interests of their nations, but on orders from outside.

The Comintern was founded after the First World War, when the Communist Parties were still weak, when practically no ties existed between the working classes of the different countries, and when the Communist Parties had not yet produced generally recognized leaders of the labor movement. The service performed by the Comintern was that it restored and strengthened the ties between the working people of the different countries, that it elaborated theoretical questions of the labor movement in the new, postwar conditions of development, that it established general standards of propaganda of the ideas of Communism, and that it facilitated the preparation of leaders of the labor movement. This created the conditions for the conver-

From *For a Lasting Peace, For a People's Democracy!*, November 10, 1947.

sion of the young Communist Parties into mass labor parties. But once the young Communist Parties had become mass labor parties, the direction of these parties from one center became impossible and inexpedient. As a result, the Comintern, from a factor promoting the development of the Communist Parties began to turn into a factor hindering their development. The new stage in the development of the Communist Parties demanded new forms of contact among the parties. It was these considerations that made it necessary to dissolve the Comintern and to devise new forms of connection between the parties.

In the course of the four years that have elapsed since the dissolution of the Comintern, the Communist Parties have grown considerably in strength and influence in nearly all the countries of Europe and Asia. The influence of the Communist Parties has increased not only in Eastern Europe, but in practically all European countries where fascism held sway, as well as in those which were occupied by the German fascists—France, Belguim, Holland, Norway, Denmark, Finland, etc. The influence of the Communists has increased especially in the new democracies, where the Communist Parties are among the most influential parties in the state.

But the present position of the Communist Parties has its shortcomings. Some comrades understood the dissolution of the Comintern to imply the elimination of all ties, of all contact, between the fraternal Communist Parties. But experience has shown that such mutual isolation of the Communist Parties is wrong, harmful and, in point of fact, unnatural. The Communist movement develops within national frameworks, but there are tasks and interests common to the parties of various countries. We get a rather curious state of affairs: the Socialists, who stopped at nothing to prove that the Comintern dictated directives from Moscow to the Communists of all countries, have restored their International; yet the Communists even refrained from meeting one another, let alone consulting with one another on questions of mutual interest to them, from fear of the slanderous talk of their enemies regarding the "hand of Moscow." Representatives of the most diverse fields of endeavor—scientists, cooperators, trade unionists, the youth, students—deem it possible to maintain international contact, to exchange experience and consult with one another on matters relating to their work, to arrange international congresses and conferences, yet the Communists, even of countries that are bound together as allies, hesitate to establish friendly ties. There can be no doubt that if the situation were to continue it would be fraught with the most serious consequences to the development of the work of the fraternal parties. The need for mutual consultation and voluntary coordination of action between individual parties has become particularly urgent at the present juncture when continued isolation may lead to a slackening of mutual understanding, and at times, even to serious blunders. . . .

The
Soviet-Yugoslav Dispute

DOCUMENT 4

*Letter from the Central Committee of the
Communist Party of Yugoslavia to the
Central Committee of the Communist
Party of the Soviet Union,
April 13, 1948.*

SHOULD WE BE asked whether we have any grounds for being discontented in our relations with you, we would have to answer openly that there are several reasons for discontent. What are these reasons? It would be impossible to expound all these reasons in this letter, yet we will quote some of them. First, we consider it incorrect that officers of the Soviet Intelligence Service should enlist our citizens in our country whilst we proceed towards socialism, and enlist them for purposes of an Intelligence Service. We are unable to give it another interpretation than by supposing it as being directed against our country's interests. This is being done despite the fact

From *The Correspondence between the Central Committee of the Communist Party of Jugoslavia and the Central Committee of the All-Union Communist Party (Bolsheviks)* (Belgrade: Jugoslovenska Knjiga, 1948). Previous letters of March 20 and 27 and subsequent letters of May 17 and 22, 1948, in the Soviet-Yugoslav exchange, not excerpted in the present anthology, appear in the book cited or in the similar book, *The Soviet-Yugoslav Dispute* (London: Royal Institute of International Affairs, 1948).

that our leadership and our officers of State Security have protested against this activity, and have let it be known that we are not willing to tolerate this any longer. Our officers are being enlisted into the Soviet Intelligence Service, our leading officials, and also all those who are inspired by hostile intentions towards the new Yugoslavia.

We possess evidence showing that some officials of the Soviet Intelligence Service, while enlisting our party members, besmirch our leaders with suspicions, belittle their prestige, and show them as incapable of their tasks and as suspicious characters. For instance, Colonel Stepanov did not hesitate, even in 1945, to try to enlist one of our good comrades who was working in the central department of cyphers and deciphering messages in our offices of State Security. Colonel Stepanov at this occasion blackened and suspected all of our leading men. He admitted, however, that "for the time being Marshal Tito is working as he should." Such cases are still to be found right up to the present. This means that such enlisting does not serve the aim of a struggle against some capitalist country. Thus we could not avoid coming to the conclusion that this activity serves the purpose of ruining our unity at home; that it is meant to destroy all confidence in the leadership; that it is carried out in order to demoralize the people, and to compromise their respect for the State leadership; and it results in producing a source of the collection of false information. This sort of activity performed by the officers of the Soviet Intelligence Service could not be regarded as being loyal and friendly disposed towards our country which is entering upon socialism and is the truest of allies of the U.S.S.R. . . .

It is obvious that the U.S.S.R. as well as Yugoslavia are vitally interested in the closest possible ties. To this end, complete mutual confidence is required. Without it no enduring and firm relations between the two countries could possibly exist. Soviet officers, and particularly leading ones, should be convinced that the New Yugoslavia, under its present leadership, is proceeding towards socialism without any hesitating on the road.

Furthermore, they should be firmly convinced that the U.S.S.R. has acquired a most true friend and ally in modern Yugoslavia under the present leadership. And this ally is ready to share good and bad days with the peoples of the U.S.S.R. in the case of heavy trials.

Finally, although we are aware of the great difficulties which the U.S.S.R. encounters in its rebuilding of its destroyed country, we feel entitled to expect assistance from the U.S.S.R. in the reconstruction of our country and in the fulfillment of the Five Year Plan. This would not entail material disadvantages to the peoples of the U.S.S.R. since it would, according to our view, be to the advantage of the U.S.S.R. if the new Yugoslavia were as strong as possible, as she is situated in direct proximity to the capitalist world which threatens not only Yugoslav peaceful development, but that of all other countries of People's Democracy, thus also that of the U.S.S.R.

Following from this the plenary meeting of the CC of the CPY are unable to consider as justified the appraisal which you have given in your letter of the work of our party and its leadership. We are deeply convinced that his constitutes a difficult misunderstanding which should have been avoided and which should be eliminated as fast as possible in the interests of the cause which our party is serving.

It is our sole desire to avoid any suspicion and any lack of confidence that is cast upon the purity of the comradely and brotherly sentiments of loyalty that inspire our CC of the CPY in respect to the All-Union Communist Party (Bolsheviks) [A-UCP (B), renamed Communist Party of the Soviet Union, 1952—ED.]. We shall always remain grateful to that party for its Marxist-Leninist teaching that has guided us up to now and shall guide us in future as well. These sentiments of loyalty inspire us also towards the Soviet Union, a country which in the past and in the future is guiding us as a great example, and the assistance which it has given to our peoples we so highly esteem.

We are convinced that this misunderstanding between us could be cleared up only through an allembracing mutual explanation to be carried out by the two Central Committees on the spot, i.e., in our country.

To that end we suggest that the CC of the A-UCP (B) send one or several of its members to our country where they will have all opportunities of investigating any question in full detail.

We conclude in the hope that our suggestion will be accepted, and convey to you our comradely greetings.

On orders of the CC of the CPY
Tito,
Kardelj.

DOCUMENT 5

Letter from the Central Committee of
the Communist Party of the Soviet Union
to the Central Committee of the Communist
Party of Yugoslavia, May 4, 1948.

WE RECEIVED YOUR reply and the communication on the decision taken at plenary session of the CC of CPY, dated 13th April, 1948, and signed by Comrades Tito and Kardelj. . . .

Particularly worthy of attention is the tone of the documents which could only be qualified as exaggeratedly ambitious. In the documents there is no desire for the truth to be clearly demonstrated, and no indication that the authors honestly admit their errors, or that they admit that these errors must be corrected and liquidated without fail. The Yugoslav comrades do not accept criticism in a Marxist manner but in the manner of small middle class people, that is to say, they receive it as an offense which lowers the prestige of the CC of the CPY and which touch the ambitions of the Yugoslav leadership.

In order to save themselves from the unenviable position into which the Yugoslav leaders have brought themselves, they take refuge in a "new" method—a method of sheer naked denial of all errors, despite the obvious nature of these. They refute all the facts so well known to them and the documentary evidence as exposed in the letter of the CC of the A-UCP (B) dated 27th March, 1948. Comrades Tito and Kardelj, evidently, do not grasp that this infantile method of naked denial of facts and documentary evidence can not convince anybody, but can only provoke laughter. . . .

In their letter dated 13th April, 1948, Comrades Tito and Kardelj write:

> We are of the opinion that he (the Soviet Ambassador) being an ambassador has no right to ask for reports on the work of our Party from whomever he wishes; this being not his job.

We are of opinion that this statement made by Comrades Tito and Kardelj is fundamentally incorrect and anti-Soviet (in spirit). As is obvious, they consider the Soviet Ambassador, a responsible Communist who in Yugoslavia represents the Communist Government of the U.S.S.R. to the Yugoslav Communist Government, as being on the same scale as any of the

From *The Correspondence between the Central Committee of the Communist Party of Jugoslavia and the Central Committee of the All-Union Communist Party (Bolsheviks)* (Belgrade: Jugoslovenska Knjiga, 1948).

bourgeois ambassadors, as being the same as any of the common officials of a bourgeois State, whose duty it is to undermine the foundations of the Yugoslav State. It is most difficult to imagine how Comrades Tito and Kardelj could possibly achieve such a degree of nonsense. Do they not grasp that such a relationship with the Soviet Ambassador means the same as the denial of friendly relations between the U.S.S.R. and Yugoslavia? Do they not grasp that the Soviet Ambassador, a responsible Communist, the representative of a friendly country which freed Yugoslavia from the German occupation, has the right, and more so the duty of entering from time to time into conversation with Communists in Yugoslavia to discuss with them all sorts of questions which might be of interest to them? How can one cover with suspicion such simple and elementary matters if one is to remain in a position of friendly relationship towards the Soviet Union? . . .

We hold that such behavior of the Yugoslav comrades towards the Soviet Ambassador could not be considered as accidental. This behavior results from a general disposition of the Yugoslav Government, whereby the Yugoslav leaders often do not see the difference between the foreign policy of the Soviet Government and that of the Anglo-Americans, and thus they identify the Soviet foreign policy with the foreign policy of the British and the Americans. And they are of opinion that Yugoslavia must conduct the same policy towards the Soviet Union as she is conducting towards the imperialist States, towards Great Britain and the U.S.A. . . .

We have mentioned in our letter that in the Yugoslav Communist Party there is not noticeable any spirit of a policy of a class struggle, that both in the village and in the town capitalist elements are on the increase and that the leadership of the Party do not take measures to hold these capitalist elements in check.

Comrades Tito and Kardelj deny all this in naked words and consider our assertion, which is based on principle, as being a sort of insult addressed to the Yugoslav Communist Party, and thereby they avoid giving an essential answer to this assertion. Their evidence could be understood as being only statements on the fundamental nature and cogency of the social transformations that have obtained in Yugoslavia. Yet this is utterly insufficient. The fact that capitalist elements are increasing in strength, and that connected with this there is an increase in the fierceness of the class struggle in the village under conditions prevailing in contemporary Yugoslavia, that is what they deny. And their negation derives from an opportunist policy according to which the class struggle in the transitory period from capitalism to socialism is alleged not to increase in fierceness, which is taught by Marxism—Leninism, but that the class struggle gets less and less as according to the opportunist school of the Bukharin type who have preached the rotten theory about capitalist elements peacefully growing into socialism. . . .

We have stated in our last letter that in Yugoslavia they consider not the Communist party, but the National Front, as the fundamental leading force, and that the Yugoslav leaders lessen the role of the party and in fact they diffuse the party into the non-party National Front. Thus in this manner they commit as much an error in principle as the Mensheviks committed in Russia 40 years ago.

Comrades Tito and Kardelj deny this and assert that all decisions of the National Front are decisions made by the party, but that they do not consider it necessary to point out in what way this or that decision was made at this or that party conference.

Yet this is just where the prime sin of the Yugoslav comrades rests, i.e., that they fear to bring the party into the open and to show its decisions everywhere, in front of the whole people, in order to acquaint the people with the leading force, namely the party, and with the fact that the party is leading the National Front, and not vice versa. . . .

In our first letter we have stated that the Communist Party in Yugoslavia has remained in a semilegal position despite the fact that it came into power three and a half years ago, also that inside the party there is no inner-party democracy, that there were no elections held, that there is no criticism, and no self-criticism, and that the CC of the CPY is composed in its majority of co-opted, and not of elected members. . . .

We are of the opinion that such an abnormal state of affairs in the Yugoslav Communist Party represents a most serious danger for the life and the development of the party. The sooner there is put an end to this sectarian-bureaucratic regime in the party, the better it will be for the CPY as well as for the Yugoslav Peoples' Democratic Republic, too. . . .

Comrades Tito and Kardelj suggest in their letter that a representative of the CC of the A-UCP (B) should be sent to Yugoslavia so that he may there study the question of Soviet-Yugoslav disagreement. We consider this suggestion as an incorrect way of dealing with the question since it is not a matter of verifying single facts because transgressions of principles are involved.

As is well known, the central committees of nine Communist parties are already acquainted with the problem of the Soviet-Yugoslav disagreement. They are in the Informbureau. It would be incorrect to exclude the other Communist parties from this matter. Therefore, we suggest that this question be discussed at the next meeting of the Inform Buro.

The CC of the A-UCP (B).

DOCUMENT 6

Statement of the Central Committee
of the Communist Party of Yugoslavia to the
Cominform Conference, June 20, 1948.

. . . THE CC OF the CPY points out that it proposed to the CC of the CPSU that it send its representatives to Yugoslavia for a joint investigation of disputed questions on the spot. The CC of the CPSU did not accept this procedure, which in our opinion represents the only correct one, but, even before receiving our answer, laid the disagreements before the other Parties of the Informbureau, that is, it sent them the text of the letter at the same time it was sent to us, at which the leaders of all the Parties, except the French and Italian, sent us written statements informing us of their judgment of our Party.

Such behavior is not in the spirit of understanding or according to the principle of voluntariness upon which the Informbureau is based.

The CC of the CPY continues to adhere to its conviction that joint discussion of disputed questions by direct contact between the CC of the CPSU and the CC of the CPY in Yugoslavia itself is the correct way to solve the existing disagreements. The CC of the CPY expresses its deep sorrow at the fact that the disagreements have taken such a form on the part of the CC of the CPSU, and again appeals, both to the CC of the CPSU and to the Informbureau, that they agree with our opinion regarding the necessity for direct contact between the CC of the CPSU and the CC of the CPY for the solution of disagreements, and to this end to remove from the agenda the discussion of the situation in our Party, comprehending the incorrectness of such discussion without our consent.

The CC of the CPY greets the brotherly Communist Parties and declares that no disagreements will prevent the CPY from remaining true to its policy of solidarity and of the closest cooperation with the CC of the CPSU and other Communist Parties.

Politbureau, CC of the CPY.

From *The Soviet-Yugoslav Dispute* (London: Royal Institute of International Affairs, 1948), pp. 59-60. Reprinted by permission of the publisher.

DOCUMENT 7

*Cominform Resolution on "The Situation
in the Communist Party of Yugoslavia,"
June, 1948.*

THE INFORMATION BUREAU, composed of the representatives of the Bulgarian Workers' Party (Communists), Rumanian Workers' Party, Hungarian Workers' Party, Polish Workers' Party, The Communist Party of the Soviet Union (Bolsheviks), Communist Party of France, Communist Party of Czechoslovakia, and the Communist Party of Italy, upon discussing the situation in the Communist Party of Yugoslavia and announcing that the representatives of the Communist Party of Yugoslavia had refused to attend the meeting of the Information Bureau, unanimously reached the following conclusions:

1. The Information Bureau notes that recently the leadership of the Communist Party of Yugoslavia has pursued an incorrect line on the main questions of home and foreign policy, a line which represents a departure from Marxism-Leninism. In this connection the Information Bureau approves the action of the Central Committee of the A-UCP (B), which took the initiative in exposing this incorrect policy of the Central Committee of the Communist Party of Yugoslavia, particularly the incorrect policy of Comrades Tito, Kardelj, Djilas and Rankovic. . . .

The Information Bureau unanimously concludes that by their anti-Party and anti-Soviet views, incompatible with Marxism-Lenininsm, by their whole attitude and their refusal to attend the meeting of the Information Bureau, the leaders of the Communist Party of Yugoslavia have placed themselves in opposition to the Communist Parties affiliated to the Information Bureau, have taken the path of seceding from the united socialist front against imperialism, have taken the path of betraying the cause of international solidarity of the working people, and have taken up a position of nationalism.

The Information Bureau condemns this anti-Party policy and attitude of the Central Committee of the Communist Party of Yugoslavia.

The Information Bureau considers that, in view of all this, the Central Committee of the Communist Party of Yugoslavia has placed itself and the Yugoslav Party outside the family of the fraternal Communist Parties, outside the united Communist front and consequently outside the ranks of the Information Bureau.

From *For a Lasting Peace, For a People's Democracy!*, July 1, 1948.

The Information Bureau considers that the basis of these mistakes made by the leadership of the Communist Party of Yugoslavia lies in the undoubted fact that nationalist elements, which previously existed in a disguised form, managed in the course of the past five or six months to reach a dominant position in the leadership of the Communist Party of Yugoslavia, and that consequently the leadership of the Yugoslav Communist Party has broken with the international traditions of the Communist Party of Yugoslavia and has taken the road of nationalism. . . .

The Yugoslav leaders evidently do not understand or, probably, pretend they do not understand, that such a nationalist line can only lead to Yugoslavia's degeneration into an ordinary bourgeois republic, to the loss of its independence and to its transformation into a colony of the imperialist countries.

The Information Bureau does not doubt that inside the Communist Party of Yugoslavia there are sufficient healthy elements, loyal to Marxism-Leninism, to the international traditions of the Yugoslav Communist Party and to the united socialist front.

Their task is to compel their present leaders to recognize their mistakes openly and honestly and to rectify them; to break with nationalism, return to internationalism; and in every way to consolidate the united socialist front against imperialism.

Should the present leaders of the Yugoslav Communist Party prove incapable of doing this, their job is to replace them and to advance a new internationalist leadership of the Party.

The Information Bureau does not doubt that the Communist Party of Yugoslavia will be able to fulfill this honorable task.

[Signed: 21 representatives
of Cominform member parties.]

DOCUMENT 8

*Cominform Resolution on "The Communist
Party of Yugoslavia in the Power of
Murderers and Spies," November, 1949.*

THE INFORMATION BUREAU, consisting of representatives of the Communist Party of Bulgaria, Rumanian Workers' Party, Working People's Party of

From *For a Lasting Peace, For a People's Democracy!*, November 29, 1949.

Hungary, United Workers' Party of Poland, Communist Party of the Soviet Union (Bolsheviks), Communist Party of France, and the Czechoslovak and Italian Communist Parties, having considered the question "The Yugoslav Communist Party in the power of muderers ond spies," unanimously reached the following conclusions:

Whereas, in June 1948 the meeting of the Information Bureau of the Communist Parties noted the changeover of the Tito-Rankovic clique from democracy and socialism to bourgeois nationalism, during the period that has elapsed since the meeting of the Information Bureau this clique has travelled all the way from bourgeois nationalism to fascism and outright betrayal of the national interests of Yugoslavia.

Recent events show that the Yugoslav Government is completely dependent on foreign imperialist circles and has become an instrument of their aggressive policy, which has resulted in the liquidation of the independence of the Yugoslav Republic.

The Central Committee of the Party and the Government of Yugoslavia have merged completely with the imperialist circles against the entire camp of socialism and democracy; against the Communist Parties of the world; against the New Democracies, and the U.S.S.R.

The Belgrade clique of hired spies and murderers made a flagrant deal with imperialist reaction and entered its service, as the Budapest trial of Rajk—Brankov made perfectly clear.

This trial showed that the present Yugoslav rulers, having fled from the camp of democracy and socialism to the camp of capitalism and reaction, have become direct accomplices of the instigators of a new war, and, by their treacherous deeds, are ingratiating themselves with the imperialists and kowtowing to them. . . .

The brutality with which staunch fighters for Communism are being annihilated in Yugoslavia, can be compared only with the atrocities of the Hitler fascists or the butcher Tsaldaris in Greece or Franco in Spain.

Expelling from the ranks of the Party those Communists loyal to proletarian internationalism, annihilating them, the Yugoslav fascists opened wide the doors of the Party to bourgeois and kulak elements.

As a result of the fascist terror of the Tito gangs against the healthy forces in the Yugoslav Communist Party, leadership of the party is wholly in the hands of spies and murderers, mercenaries of imperialism.

The Information Bureau of Communist and Workers' Parties considers therefore, that the struggle against the Tito clique—hired spies and murderers, is the international duty of all Communist and Workers' Parties.

It is the duty of Communist and Workers' Parties to give all possible aid to the Yugoslav working class and working peasantry who are fighting for the return of Yugoslavia to the camp of democracy and socialism.

A necessary condition for the return of Yugoslavia to the socialist camp is active struggle on the part of revolutionary elements both inside the Yugoslav Communist Party and outside its ranks, for the regeneration of the revolutionary, genuine Communist Party of Yugoslavia, loyal to Marxism-Leninism, to the principles of proletarian internationalism, and fighting for the independence of Yugoslavia from imperialism.

The loyal Communist forces in Yugoslavia who, in the present brutal conditions of fascist terror, are deprived of the possibility of engaging in open action against the Tito-Rankovic clique, were compelled in the struggle for the cause of Communism, to follow the path taken by the Communists of those countries where legal work is forbidden.

The Information Bureau expresses the firm conviction that, among the workers and peasants of Yugoslavia, forces will be found capable of ensuring victory over the bourgeois-restoration espionage Tito-Rankovic clique; that the toiling people of Yugoslavia led by the working class will succeed in restoring the historical gains of People's Democracy, won at the price of heavy sacrifice and heroic struggle by the peoples of Yugoslavia, and that they will take the road of building socialism. . . .

[Signed by 22 representatives
of Cominform member parties.]

The
Sino-Soviet Alliance

DOCUMENT 9

"Treaty of Friendship, Alliance and Mutual Assistance," February 14, 1950.

THE PRESIDIUM OF the Supreme Soviet of the Union of Soviet Socialist Republics and the Central People's Government of the People's Republic of China;

Filled with determination jointly to prevent, by the consolidation of friendship and cooperation between the Union of Soviet Socialist Republics and the People's Republic of China, the rebirth of Japanese imperialism and a repetition of aggression on the part of Japan or any other State which should unite in any form with Japan in acts of aggression;

Imbued with the desire to consolidate lasting peace and universal security in the Far East and throughout the world in conformity with the aims and principles of the United Nations Organization;

Profoundly convinced that the consolidation of good-neighborly relations and friendship between the Union of Soviet Socialist Republics and the People's Republic of China meets the fundamental interests of the peoples of the Soviet Union and China;

Resolved for this purpose to conclude the present Treaty and appointed as their plenipotentiary representatives . . . [Vyshinsky and Chou En-lai] . . . ;

Who, after exchange of their credentials, found in due form and good order, agreed upon the following:

Article I

Both High Contracting Parties undertake jointly to take all the necessary measures at their disposal for the purpose of preventing a repetition of aggression and violation of peace on the part of Japan or any other State which should unite with Japan, directly or indirectly, in acts of aggression.

From *Soviet News,* February 15, 1950.

In the event of one of the High Contracting Parties being attacked by Japan or States allied with it, and thus being involved in a state of war, the other High Contracting Party will immediately render military and other assistance with all the means at its disposal.

The High Contracting Parties also declare their readiness in the spirit of sincere cooperation, to participate in all international actions aimed at ensuring peace and security throughout the world, and will do all in their power to achieve the speediest implementation of these tasks.

Article II

Both the High Contracting Parties undertake by means of mutual agreement to strive for the earliest conclusion of a peace treaty with Japan, jointly with the other Powers which were allies during the Second World War.

Article III

Both High Contracting Parties undertake not to conclude any alliance directed against the other High Contracting Party, and not to take part in any coalition or in actions or measures directed against the other High Contracting Party.

Article IV

Both High Contracting Parties will consult each other in regard to all important international problems affecting the common interests of the Soviet Union and China, being guided by the interests of the consolidation of peace and universal security.

Article V

Both the High Contracting Parties undertake, in the spirit of friendship and cooperation and in conformity with the principles of equality, mutual interests, and also mutual respect for the State sovereignty and territorial integrity and non-interference in internal affairs of the other High Contracting Party—to develop and consolidate economic and cultural ties between the Soviet Union and China, to render each other every possible economic assistance, and to carry out the necessary economic cooperation.

Article VI

The present Treaty comes into force immediately upon its ratification; the exchange of instruments of ratification will take place in Peking.

The present Treaty will be valid for 30 years. If neither of the High Contracting Parties gives notice one year before the expiration of this term of its desire to denounce the Treaty, it shall remain in force for another five years and will be extended in compliance with this rule. . . .

[Signed by A. Ia. Vyshinsky and Chou En-lai.]

II

COMMONWEALTH

AND

CONFRONTATION, 1954–1960

After the death of Stalin, the feudal overlord of Communism, in 1953, international relations among Communists were at first deceptively calm. The funeral of the great dictator provided a fine symbolic expression of fraternity among party leaders, many of whom gathered in Moscow, but at this time nobody seems to have wished to raise fundamental questions concerning the international Communist order. Perhaps it was an unsurpassed tribute to the dominating spirit of the departed that the habits of docility that he had tried to inculcate held up for some time even in his absence. Yet his Soviet heirs, preoccupied as they were with internal problems of political succession, economic reforms, and relaxation of the police state, apparently realized that relations with foreign Communist parties and states had to be modified, too. While they seem to have gravely underestimated the complexities and pitfalls in this matter, it is to their credit that the initiative for reform in the international field was largely theirs until 1956.

At first the Soviet leaders had no dramatic new approach to the international Communist problem, but seem to have felt that the Soviet-centered, inherited system could be put on a stable footing through reasonableness in bilateral negotiations. China was promised more economic aid as early as May, 1953, and in October, 1954, Khrushchev and Mikoyan went to Peking and agreed to a further increase in credits, to the end of the objectionable joint companies, and to the return to China of Port Arthur and Darien. The European satellites also benefitted by the sale to them of the joint companies. Another organizational reform was the institution of the Warsaw Treaty (Document 10), which was presented to the satellite governments at a meeting in Moscow in November, 1954, and signed in Warsaw on May 14, 1955. This did not alter the fact of Soviet military presence and Soviet control of satellite armies, but provided a new appearance of legality and a basis for durability. The clause concerning the establishment of a joint command even suggested a new degree of mutuality, but in practice Marshal Konev's Soviet command was simply renamed.

Some other forms of de-Stalinization in Eastern Europe involved direct Soviet intervention in the internal affairs of the satellite parties and states with the same degree of authoritarianism that the late dictator had applied. For example, Rakosi, the tyrannical party secretary and premier of Hungary, was summoned to Moscow in June, 1953, to receive sharp reproaches for concentrating so much power in his own hands—a ludicrous criticism in view of the obvious point that Rakosi had merely been following Stalin's example. With scant concern for Hungarian integrity, he was sent home with orders to transfer the premiership to Imre Nagy, whom he detested. With somewhat less acrimony similar divisions of party and state command were imposed on Poland, Czechoslovakia, Rumania, and Bulgaria in the early post-Stalin phase.

The most strikingly un-Stalinist measure that the Soviet leadership undertook was the reconciliation with the "spies, murderers and mercenaries of imperialism" in Yugoslavia. Khrushchev, the Soviet party secretary but not yet an unchallenged ruler, was the main proponent of this policy. It is hard to know just how he envisaged the prospects. Yugoslavia as an outcast could not threaten the security of the U.S.S.R., and the Eastern European satellites seemed successfully insulated from Tito's influence. On the other hand, any reconciliation had to be based on truly equitable negotiations that would set dangerous precedent for international Communist relations in Europe, with incalculable effects on other satellite regimes. But the traditional appeal of a united, fraternal coalition of all Communists seems to have been irresistible. At about the same time that active overtures to Tito were undertaken, the Soviet ideological organ, *Kommunist* (no. 14, 1955), underscored the need for unity by advancing the concept of a "commonwealth [*sodruzhestvo*] of socialist states." Although the content of this label was not elaborated upon, it seems to be associated with the optimistic belief that Communists could form a solid league on the basis of such voluntary cohesion as would satisfy the Yugoslav leaders.

In any case, Khrushchev worked hard to overcome domestic opposition and Tito's caution, while ignoring the helpless unhappiness that the reconciliation caused among other Eastern European Communist leaders. In June, 1955, Khrushchev and Premier Bulganin made a formal visit to Tito in Belgrade, lamely blaming the dead police boss Beria for the rupture in 1948. Khrushchev succeeded in restoring normal interstate relations but not interparty relations. In the following 12 months other steps were taken: alleged

Titoists were rehabilitated (posthumously, or alive in the case of the fortunate Gomulka); Stalin's policy toward Tito was denounced in Khrushchev's secret speech to the Twentieth Congress of the Soviet party in February, 1956; and the Cominform was dissolved (Document 11). Impressed by these overtures and eager to influence the development of Eastern European Communism, Tito was happy to go to Moscow in June, 1956, and approve the formal renewal of interparty relations with the Soviet Communists (Document 12), and, in consequence, with the parties under its leadership.

But Khrushchev had seriously underestimated the difficulties that faced the "commonwealth." When he chose to attack Stalin before the party congress of February, 1956, he seems to have had mainly domestic considerations in mind, and, except for the Yugoslav issue, skirted problems of international Communist relations. But Stalin had been much more than a Soviet leader. He had been a mythological giant of all faithful Communists in his day, and the demolition of his image was to have far-reaching results in interparty relations. In countries without Communist governments, where Communist party members were not subject to police discipline, the discrediting of Stalin posed a threat to the formerly Stalinist party leaders. Their obedience seems to have been taken for granted in the post-Stalin groping toward a "commonwealth," and they were not informed of the attack on Stalin until after it had been delivered. Of all the dismayed reactions, the most notable was that of the old Comintern employee Togliatti. Coining the term "polycentrism" (Document 13), he in effect served notice that the former obedience to Moscow died with the old image of Stalin. The Chinese Communist leadership was for several years more circumspect in commenting on the affair, but in time made it clear that they strongly objected to both the appraisal of Stalin and to the unilateral way in which it was done.

But it was in Poland and Hungary that the end of the Stalin-myth had its most turbulent repercussions. Infused with a new spirit of daring, encouraged indirectly by the Yugoslavs and the Chinese, and pressed by a mutinous population, the anti-Stalin wing of the Polish Communist Party arranged to supplant the old leadership with a group of its own choosing, headed by Gomulka. This challenge to the authority of the Soviet Union evidently exceeded Khrushchev's idea of what was permissible within a "commonwealth," and he headed a prestigious Soviet delegation that flew uninvited to Warsaw on October 19, 1956, to force the Poles to coordinate their internal changes with Soviet desires (the Poles having dodged an invitation to come to Moscow for this purpose). In this crucial negotiation the new Polish Communist leaders at once assured the Soviet Union of their basic loyalty as allies and insisted that the Soviets grant some real sovereignty to the Polish party and state. Rather than risk an unsightly war of repression, the Soviet leaders accepted the Polish position and on November 18 negotiated a general agreement on the terms of the new relationship (Document 16).

In Hungary there were greater complications. No Communist party had been treated more highhandedly than the Hungarian, and the Soviet-Yugoslav reconciliation had the immediate affect of emphasizing this. Tito was bent on securing the complete removal of Stalin's Hungarian toady Rakosi, and hoped to play patron to the reformed Hungarian Communist regime. Khrushchev seemed willing to exchange this extension of Yugoslav influence for Tito's friendship, Rakosi was obliged to resign in July, 1956, and on October 15-22 Tito established a close bilateral relationship with the new Hungarian party boss, Gerö. But Gerö was merely a maladroit Stalinist, and appears to have determined to provoke a small public disorder to provide justification for a major police campaign against advocates of liberalization, whom he feared. A demonstration in Budapest on October 23, in sympathy with the new Polish government, provided Gerö with a pretext for repression, but unexpectedly led to a massive popular upheaval, supported by the armed forces. In the ensuing turmoil unilateral Soviet military intervention proved inadequate to pacify Budapest, an anti-Stalinist Communist, Imre Nagy, became premier, and a somewhat equivocal figure, Kadar, took over as first secretary of the party. Not only reformist Communists, but also powerful anti-Communist forces had been released, and not only the Soviet Union but also the adjacent, independent Communist governments were alarmed. For Tito and Gomulka either Soviet repression or the emergence of a non-Communist Hungary was an unsettling prospect, and they tried in vain to persuade the Hungarians to restrain their revolution (Document 14). The Soviets, too, tried to assure the Hungarians—and other former satellites that might be tempted to follow their example—that the socialist commonwealth would not resemble the Stalinist pattern of inter-Communist relations. On October 30, the Soviet government published new "Principles of Development and Further Strengthening of Friendship and Cooperation Between the Soviet Union and Other Socialist States" (Document 15). But the liberalizing and nationalistic pressures in Hungary were powerful and the Communist premier Nagy was willing to cooperate with them. Multiparty government was reestablished, free elections promised, and the four-party cabinet determined on with withdrawal from the Warsaw Treaty Organization in protest against ominous Soviet troop movements. These movements were in fact preparatory to a full-scale military attack on the Hungarian revolution, still headed by an avowedly Communist premier, but one no longer recognized as such by the Kremlin. Instead, the Soviet

Union shifted its party and state recognition to Kadar, whom they had removed to Soviet territory and who returned to Budapest as party secretary and premier in the baggage train of the Red Army, which launched its final drive on November 4. At this point international relations between the Soviet Union and Hungary ceased to exist in any meaningful sense, and revived only gradually as Soviet military government was replaced by the Hungarian Communist regime of Kadar.

Despite the ruthlessness of the Soviet repressions and its deadening affect on the image of a Communist commonwealth, Khrushchev persisted in his efforts to consolidate international Communist unity on the basis of consensus. The years 1957-1960 saw a series of steps in this direction, with multilateral forms increasingly employed. However, the Soviet Union was no longer the only power exercising initiative among the Communists. In early 1957 Premier Chou En-lai of China made a tour of the Eastern European Communist countries, implicitly staking the Chinese claim to universal and direct interest in inter-Communist relations. Although there was no apparent effort to organize a non-Soviet faction of Communist states, the warmth of the Polish response to the Chinese (Document 17) initiative indicated that there were European Communist leaders who welcomed this trend toward polycentrism. Not all non-Soviet party leaders did so. The conservative Communist leadership of Czechoslovakia took pains to meet with Thorez, the old-line French boss, in January, 1957, and denounce the "idea that there can be several centers of international Communist movement," which was in keeping with concurrent Soviet stress on the importance of "proletarian internationalism." But the very appearance of the Czech-French support for Soviet leadership in this time of insecurity was a sign of a heightened sense of freedom of choice. Certainly the Yugoslav Communists were conscious of having retained their freedom of action. While Tito acknowledged that the second, successful Soviet armed attack in Hungary had been necessary in the circumstances, and while he carried on personal diplomacy with both Gomulka and Khrushchev in the summer of 1957, the Yugoslav leader apparently considered himself an independent ideological oracle in his own right.

The main effort of the Soviet Union to pull these divergent trends together into a more tangible commonwealth was the Moscow conference of the 13 parties in power, convened in November, 1957, in honor of the fortieth anniversary of Lenin's revolution. The "Declaration" (Document 18) of this unprecedented gathering superficially represented the achievement of a consensus of the socialist commonwealth. But the concurrence of the Chinese was reluctant, possibly having been won by Khrushchev's promised delivery of a sample atomic bomb, with technical instructions, shortly before the Moscow meeting. Later, in 1963, the Chinese said that their delegation, headed by Mao Tse-tung, had compromised in accepting some passages of the final Declaration, while fighting hard and successfully to replace some of the "revisionist" portions of the original Soviet draft. The Yugoslavs would not sign the document at all, owing to its attacks on "revisionism" (implying errors in their party). The parties not in power did not object openly to their exclusion from the proceedings, but it may be relevant that in 1959 there were two conferences of Western European Communist parties: a meeting of the six parties of Common Market countries in April and a general meeting of 17 European Communist parties not in power in November. While recognizing the leadership of the Soviet Union, the resolution of the larger of these two gatherings was notable for its omission of any attack on revisionism.*

Following the Moscow conference of 1957 it was indeed the campaign against revisionism, especially the Yugoslav form, that provided a rallying point for the Communist parties of the commonwealth. Despite economic pressures, including withdrawal of Soviet aid and exclusion from the widening activities of Comecon, Yugoslavia defended her domestic policies and sovereignty, and in the spring of 1958 summarized these points in a new party program (Document 19). This drew a slashing attack from Peking, amounting to expulsion from the Communist community, and in general the Soviet Union joined in the loud blasts against revisionism. But underlying the verbal solidarity a series of disagreements between the two great powers of Communism were gaining momentum. One was the issue of tactics toward the imperialist enemy. While Khrushchev stressed the necessity of peaceful coexistence in the face of nuclear weapons and engaged in highly publicized promotion of this view in summit meetings with capitalists and at the U.N., the Chinese maintained that the revolutionary masses of the world dared risk conflict with the oppressors. While appearing to continue to single out the Yugoslav revisionists as the perpetrators of error in this matter, the major Chinese newspaper article "Long Live Leninism!" (Document 20) also referred to "well-intentioned persons who sincerely want to be Marxists but who get confused in the face of certain new historical phenomena and thus have some incorrect ideas"—a clear allusion to the Soviets and their views on nuclear weapons. This posture of superior ideological insight had as early as 1958 been displayed in connection with the domestic program of communes in China. In glorifying this massive effort to mobilize labor for agricultural and small-scale industrial projects without individual incentives, Chinese propaganda suggested that the country could

* *World Marxist Review*, no. 1, 1960, pp. 46-50.

move rapidly toward the attainment of the ultimate Communist society without a long period of economic modernization. This perspective cast doubt on the assumption that the Soviet Union had advanced closer to ultimate Communism than any other society, and perhaps even suggested that the Soviets were not very good ideological pathfinders in such a matter. Certainly Khrushchev intended a rebuttal to such aspersions when in 1959 he took up the question of Soviet progress toward Communist society at a special party congress, and again in 1961 when still another party congress adopted a new program that envisaged the beginning of a fully Communist society in 20 years. Quite a different, more stinging rebuttal was the Soviet abrogation in June, 1959, of the 1957 agreement to help China develop nuclear weapons.

These issues and some subsidiary ones, such as the noncommittal Soviet attitude toward a Sino-Indian border clash in 1959, still had not produced a face-to-face confrontation when the Rumanian Workers' Party (later renamed Communist) held its congress in Bucharest in June, 1960. Khrushchev, reacting to the Chinese article "Long Live Leninism!," sought to gain the initiative by attending the congress himself as a fraternal observer and organizing a special conference of visiting observers from many other parties. These representatives were acquainted with the Soviet version of recent Sino-Soviet relations in a long circular letter, followed up by a major speech by Khrushchev on the subject (Document 21). Perhaps Khrushchev was confident that he had isolated the Chinese and could proceed to enforce their capitulation to Soviet leadership by one swift blow to their vulnerable economy, by withdrawing on very short notice all Soviet technological personnel in China and the blueprints of Soviet-supported projects. Since this move was an inexcusable violation of earlier state agreements, Khrushchev could hardly have expected the Chinese to be pleased, but he may well have expected them to be more submissive. If such was the case, the Soviet dictator must have been exceedingly disappointed, for the Chinese responded in September with a circular letter of their own and at the end of that month began a dogged defense of their views in a prolonged meeting of delegates from 26 parties in Moscow in October, 1960. The goal of this conference was the composition of a general "Statement" that almost all Communist parties could agree to at a world-wide meeting, a festival of solidarity which was intended to create a new consensus. In November, the "Statement" did emerge (Document 22), duly signed by the 81 parties that attended (which the Yugoslavs did not). Judging from subsequent revelations by Western European participants, the disagreements that came out in the course of the debates were so strong that it is a wonder that the document emerged at all. Not only did the two main antagonists have their bitter differences, but a host of other parties evidently had their own ideas to present. The Brazilian and Cuban parties (the latter appearing as the proprietor of the newest Communist state) proposed an amendment condemning factional activities. The French party leader Thorez proposed a compromise formula on "voluntary unity" to cover the sensitive question of authority and discipline in the movement. The leading Italian delegate Longo resisted efforts "to isolate Yugoslavia from the workers' movement." The Albanian party leader Hoxha, who had been having increasing differences with the Soviets concerning economic aid and the selection of leaders in Albania, spoke out sharply in favor of the general position of China and angrily walked out of the whole affair. And some other representatives, including the Soviets, unsuccessfully proposed that an international secretariat be established. In sum, the Moscow conference of 81 parties of November 1960 was a real confrontation of diverse opinions, not the kind of sham-parliament that many Communist representative bodies have been. In a liberal sense, this might be considered a real advance for true commonwealth. However, from the Communist viewpoint the affair was most striking as an ominous confrontation of the two great powers of Communism, despite the façade of unity that the compromise statement provided.

Toward
a De-Stalinized Order

DOCUMENT 10

*"Treaty of Friendship, Cooperation and
Mutual Assistance Between the People's
Republic of Albania, the People's
Republic of Bulgaria, the Hungarian
People's Republic, the German Democratic
Republic, the Rumanian People's
Republic, the Union of Soviet Socialist
Republics, and the Czechoslovak Republic,"
May 14, 1955. (Treaty of Warsaw).*

THE CONTRACTING PARTIES,*

reaffirming their desire for the establishment of a system of European
collective security based on the participation of all European states irrespective of their social and political systems, which would make it possible to
unite their efforts in safeguarding the peace of Europe;

mindful, at the same time, of the situation created in Europe by the ratification of the Paris agreements, which envisage the formation of a new
military alignment in the shape of "Western European Union," with the participation of a remilitarized Western Germany and the integration of the
latter in the North-Atlantic bloc, which increases the danger of another war
and constitutes a threat to the national security of the peaceable states;

being persuaded that in these circumstances the peaceable European
states must take the necessary measures to safeguard their security and in
the interests of preserving peace in Europe;

guided by the objects and principles of the Charter of the United Nations
Organization;

being desirous of further promoting and developing friendship, coopera-

---

From *New Times,* no. 21, 1955.

* The word "party" is here used in its legalistic sense, not with reference to Communist parties—ED.

tion and mutual assistance in accordance with the principles of respect for the independence and sovereignty of states and of non-interference in their internal affairs,

have decided to conclude the present Treaty of Friendship, Sooperation, and Mutual Assistance and have for that purpose appointed as their plenipotentiaries:

[The names of the premiers of the above countries are listed here—ED.]

who, having presented their full powers, found in good and due form, have agreed as follows:

Article 1

The Contracting Parties undertake, in accordance with the Charter of the United Nations Organization, to refrain in their international relations from the threat or use of force, and to settle their international disputes peacefully and in such manner as will not jeopardize international peace and secruity. . . .

Article 4

In the event of armed attack in Europe on one or more of the Parties to the Treaty by any state or group of states, each of the Parties to the Treaty, in the exercise of its right to individual or collective self-defense in accordance with Article 51 of the Charter of the United Nations Organization, shall immediately, either individually or in agreement with other Parties to the Treaty, come to the assistance of the state or states attacked with all such means as it deems necessary, including armed force. The Parties to the Treaty shall immediately consult concerning the necessary measures to be taken by them jointly in order to restore and maintain international peace and security.

Measures taken on the basis of this Article shall be reported to the Security Council in conformity with the provisions of the Charter of the United Nations Organization. These measures shall be discontinued immediately the Security Council adopts the necessary measures to restore and maintain international peace and security.

Article 5

The Contracting Parties have agreed to establish a Joint Command of the armed forces that by agreement among the Parties shall be assigned to the Command, which shall function on the basis of jointly established principles. They shall likewise adopt other agreed measures necessary to strengthen their defensive power, in order to protect the peaceful labors of their peoples, guarantee the inviolability of their frontiers and territories, and provide defense against possible aggression.

Article 6

For the purpose of the consultations among the Parties envisaged in the present Treaty, and also for the purpose of examining questions which may arise in the operation of the Treaty, a Political Consultative Committee shall be set up, in which each of the Parties to the Treaty shall be represented by a member of its Government or by another specifically appointed representative.

The Committee may set up such auxiliary bodies as may prove necessary.

Article 7

The Contracting Parties undertake not to participate in any coalitions or alliances and not to conclude any agreements whose objects conflict with the objects of the present Treaty.

The Contracting Parties declare that their commitments under existing international treaties do not conflict with the provisions of the present Treaty.

Article 8

The Contracting Parties declare that they will act in a spirit of friendship and cooperation with a view to further developing and fostering economic and cultural intercourse with one another, each adhering to the principle of respect for the independence and sovereignty of the others and non-interference in their internal affairs.

Article 9

The present Treaty is open to the accession of other states, irrespective of their social and political systems, which express their readiness by participation in the present Treaty to assist in uniting the efforts of the peaceable states in safeguarding the peace and security of the peoples. Such accession shall enter into force with the agreement of the Parties to the Treaty after the declaration of accession has been deposited with the Government of the Polish People's Republic.

Article 10

The present Treaty is subject to ratification, and the instruments of ratification shall be deposited with the Government of the Polish People's Republic.

The Treaty shall enter into force on the day the last instrument of ratification has been deposited. The Government of the Polish People's Republic shall notify the other Parties to the treaty as each instrument of ratification is deposited.

Article 11

The present Treaty shall remain in force for twenty years. For such Contracting Parties as do not at least one year before the expiration of this period present to the Government of the Polish People's Republic a statement of denunciation of the Treaty, it shall remain in force for the next ten years.

Should a system of collective security be established in Europe, and a General European Treaty of Collective Security concluded for this purpose, for which the Contracting Parties will unswervingly strive, the present Treaty shall cease to be operative from the day the General European Treaty enters into force. . . .

[Signed by the premiers of the participating countries.]

DOCUMENT 11

The Dissolution of the Cominform, April 17, 1956.

THE FOUNDING IN 1947 of the Information Bureau of the Communist and Workers Parties was a positive contribution toward overcoming the lack of coordination which developed among Communist Parties after the dissolution of the Comintern [in 1943] and was an important force in strengthening proletarian internationalism in the ranks of the international Communist movement and in further uniting the working class and all working people in the struggle for lasting peace, democracy, and socialism. The Information Bureau and its newspaper, *For a Lasting Peace, for a People's Democracy!,* played a positive role in developing and strengthening fraternal ties and mutual exchanges of experience among Communist and Work-

From *The Current Digest of the Soviet Press* (published weekly at Columbia University), Vol. VIII, No. 16, p. 6. © 1956 by The Joint Committee on Slavic Studies and reprinted by permission of *The Current Digest of the Soviet Press.* Originally in *Pravda,* April 18, 1956, p. 3.

ers Parties and in clarifying problems of Marxist-Leninist theory as applied to the concrete conditions in various countries and the experience of the international Communist and working class movement. This promoted the ideological, organizational, and political strengthening of the fraternal parties and an extension of the influence of Communist Parties among the masses.

However, there have been changes in recent years in the international situation: the extension of socialism beyond the boundaries of a single country and its transformation into a world system; the formation of a vast "peace zone" including both socialist and nonsocialist peace-loving countries of Europe and Asia; the growth and consolidation of many Communist Parties in capitalist, dependent, and colonial countries and their increased activities in the struggle against the threat of war and reaction, in the struggle for peace, for the vital interests of the working people and their countries' national independence; and, finally, the particularly urgent tasks today of overcoming the division within the working class movement and strengthening the unity of the working class in the interests of a successful struggle for peace and socialism. These changes have provided new conditions for the activities of the Communist and Workers Parties. The Information Bureau of the Communist and Workers Parties, in terms both of its make-up and the content of its activity, no longer meets these new conditions.

The Central Committees of the Communist and Workers Parties belonging to the Information Bureau having exchanged views on problems of its activity, recognized that the Information Bureau which they set up in 1947 had completed its function, and so by mutual agreement they adopted a decision to end the activity of the Information Bureau of the Communist and Workers Parties and its newspaper, *For a Lasting Peace, for a People's Democracy!* . . .

[Signed by the central committees of the Communist parties
of Bulgaria, Hungary, Italy, Poland,
Rumania, U.S.S.R., Czechoslovakia, France.]

DOCUMENT 12

Declaration on the Reestablishment of Relations Between the Yugoslav and Soviet Communist Parties, June 20, 1956.

IN THE COURSE of the conversations [between delegations headed by Tito and Khrushchev, meeting in Moscow during June 1-23, 1956—ED.] they agreed upon the following:

1. The Belgrade Declaration of June 2, 1955, placed relations between the two socialist countries on a healthy footing, and the principles formulated in it are finding ever broader application in their mutual cooperation.

2. Cooperation between the two countries and the general development of their relations since the signing of the Belgrade Declaration, and also the contacts established between their political and other public organizations, have created favorable political conditions for cooperation also between the CPSU and the YLC [Yugoslav League of Communists—same as Communist Party of Yugoslavia—ED.].

Proceeding from the foregoing, bearing in mind the concrete conditions of development of the modern socialist movements, and guided by the internationalist principles of Marxism-Leninism, the delegations of the YLC and CPSU have agreed on the need and value of continuously developing existing contacts between the two parties for cooperation in further strengthening our socialist countries and promoting their prosperity, for cooperation in the international labor movement on a wide range of questions concerning the present development of socialism, and also for the development of peaceful coexistence and cooperation between the nations of the world, regardless of difference in social and political systems, in the interests of the peace, freedom, and independence of the peoples.

The representatives of the two parties proceed from the premise that continued development of contacts and cooperation between the CPSU and YLC, as the leading parties in countries where the working class is in power, and as parties which share the common aim of building a complete socialist society in their countries and ensuring human progress and durable peace, will undoubtedly facilitate further cooperation between the U.S.S.R. and F.P.R.Y. [Yugoslavia] and the promotion of enduring friendship between their peoples.

3. Believing that the path of socialist development differs in various countries and conditions, that the multiplicity of forms of socialist develop-

From *New Times*, no. 26, 1956, supplement.

ment tends to strengthen socialism, and proceeding from the fact that any tendency of imposing one's opinion on the ways and forms of socialist development is alien to both—the two parties have agreed that their cooperation shall be based on complete voluntariness and equality, friendly criticism, and comradely exchange of opinions on controversial questions.

4. With the above as a basis, cooperation between the YLC and CPSU will develop primarily through comprehensive mutual acquaintance with the forms and methods of socialist construction in both countries, free and comradely exchange of experience and opinions on questions of common interest for the development of socialist practice and for the advancement of socialist thought, and also on questions concerning peace, rapprochement, and intercourse between nations, and human progress generally.

5. The present material and spiritual reconstruction of the world, which finds expression in the tremendous growth of the forces of socialism, the upsurge of the national-liberation movement, the increased part played by the working class in the solution of concrete questions of international development, poses a number of momentous tasks before the international labor movement. From this follows the need for scientific analysis of developments and of the basic material and social factors and trends in the present-day world. For these reasons the two parties have agreed that guided by the principles of Marxism-Leninism, they will do everything to encourage—both in their relations and in the international labor movement generally—mutual cooperation and exchange of opinions in the field of socialist scientfic thought.

6. With regard to concrete forms of cooperation between the YLC and the CPSU, the delegations have agreed that it will be carried out through personal contacts, written and oral communications and exchange of opinions, through exchange of delegations, information matter, and literature, as well as through personal meetings of party leaders, when necessary, to discuss pressing problems of common interest, and generally through all forms of constructive comradely discussion.

7. The representatives of the CPSU and YLC consider such cooperation to be a component part of their contacts with other Communist and Workers Parties, and also with the socialist and other progressive movements of the world.

8. The CPSU and YLC believe that the promotion of durable peace, security, and social progress requires broad cooperation between all progressive and peace-loving forces, which is making itself increasingly felt in diverse forms and on a world scale. This cooperation is an essential need of modern social development. Such contacts must be equal, frank, democratic, and accessible to world public opinion. They should serve as a

means of reciprocal information and consultation on diverse problems of general interest, and should foster closer understanding, based on tolerant explanation of the positions and views of the parties. This presupposes freedom of action for each and every participant in this cooperation, in conformity with the conditions of their development and their general progressive aims. . . .

[Signed on behalf of their respective central committees
by Tito and Khrushchev.]

DOCUMENT 13

Togliatti's Speech on "Polycentrism" to the
Central Committee of the Italian
Communist Party, June 24, 1956.

. . . WE FACE A greatly different picture from that which we encountered in the past decades, and in this picture, the problem of leadership of the movements toward socialism and of the Communist movements and parties themselves, inevitably also must be viewed differently than in the past. For us there is no doubt that the Soviet Union remains the first great historical model of conquest of power by the working class, and of utilization of this power in the most energetic and effective manner in order to succeed, once the resistence of the bourgeois and other reactionary classes was swept away and foreign attempts to intervene repelled, in readying itself for the task of constructing a new economy and society and in carrying out this task.

The experience which thus has been accomplished is an enormous experience which has its great, prevailing positive aspects and also its negative aspects. The study of this experience has been, and will continue to be, invaluable instruction not only for the Communist parties, which must always refer to it, but also for all those who wish to understand today's conditions, who aspire to economic and social changes of a radical nature, and who want to proceed toward these changes. But this experience cannot include either the ready-made solution of all the problems which today present

From The Russian Institute, Columbia University, *The Anti-Stalin Campaign and International Communism: A Selection of Documents* (New York: Columbia University Press, 1956), pp. 214-218. Reprinted by permission of the publisher.

themselves in those countries which are already ruled by the working class and by the Communist parties, or much less, the ready-made answer to the questions which arise where, instead, the Communist parties or the parties oriented toward socialism are opposition parties which move in an environment completely different from that in which moved the vanguard of the working class in Russia during and after the seizure of power. The experience accomplished in the building of a socialist society in the Soviet Union cannot contain instructions for resolving all the questions which may present themselves today to us and to the Communists of other countries, whether in power or not, and to all the vanguard parties of the working class and of the people.

Thus various points or centers of development and orientation are established. There is established what I called in the interview which you have read, a polycentric system, corresponding to the new situation, to the alteration in the world make-up and in the very structure of the workers' movements, and to this system correspond also new types of relations among the Communist parties themselves. The solution which today probably most nearly corresponds to this new situation, may be that of the full autonomy of the individual Communist parties and of bilateral relations between them to establish complete, mutual understanding and complete, mutual trust, conditions necessary for collaboration and to give unity to the Communist movement itself and to the entire progressive movement of the working class. Such a system is probably also one which can make possible a better expansion of relations between the Communist movements and the non-Communist, socialist-oriented movements (socialists, social democrats who favor national liberation, etc.); which can make it possible to face and resolve in a new way the questions of bringing together different sectors of the workers' movement, of understanding, of mutual trust, and eventually, tomorrow, of agreement among all the parties working for socialist changes in the world. Unity of action, such as we have attained in Italy with the Socialist Party and such as has been attained in other countries at other times, is one of the means by which is solved the problem of this agreement, but it is not the only possible one, even though it is among the most widely proposed.

It is evident that in this new situation, while we are working in a new way to establish contact with the other parts of the international Communist movement and with the other sectors of the socialist-oriented workers and popular movements, we are reaffirming with energy, and must struggle to intensify in our own ranks, in the working class and among the people, the spirit of proletarian internationalism. However, the more we shall succeed in achieving this aim, the more we shall succeed in giving our proletarian internationalism a precise, solid-tone substance which corresponds to the situation facing us, which does not fall into a repetition of formulas of the past, but which faces with spirit and new initiative all the problems which today may present themselves to the vanguard parties of the working class.

Faithful to this orientation, we have worked to solve and we have solved the question of our relations with the League of Yugoslav Communists. You remember the past, the errors which have been committed, the way in which these errors have been corrected, and you recall the steps which we have recently taken to re-establish normal relations with the Yugoslav Communists. My trip to Belgrade, which took place in a slightly hasty manner because on both sides it was necessary to take into account prior commitments, had been preceded by contacts between other leaders of the party and leaders of the League of Yugoslav Communists and has come to an excellent result. We have established with the League of Yugoslav Communists bilateral relations of solidarity and trust, relations which we shall develop so as to succeed in understanding even more what our Yugoslav comrades are doing, to have them understand better what we are doing, and to lend our hand, at this time and in this field, to the solution of the great problem of establishing new relations among all the sectors of the workers' movement which are marching toward socialism, each following its own path.

We especially hail the agreement recently reached between the Communist Party of the Soviet Union and the leaders of the League of Yugoslav Communists during Tito's recent trip to Moscow. I invite our comrades to read and study the text of this agreement because it seems to me that it could constitute a model for the new relations which are being set up among the different sectors of the Communist movement. [See Document 12—Ed.]

In this new situation, the relations with the Communist Party of the Soviet Union and with the great movement of the Soviet Communists appear in a new light. The treatment of this question has been partly complicated by the interference of the revelations contained in the report made by Comrade Khrushchev in a secret session of the 20th Congress.

These revelations have aroused surprise and commotion, have caused the perturbation which you know, and have given rise in our party, and I believe also in other Communist parties, to a vast debate which is still under way. Aside from this fact, the question of relations between the Communist Party of the Soviet Union and the Communist movement of other countries was making itself felt in any case. It was an objectively mature question, because the situation itself required that these relations be examined and clearly placed on a new basis. Without a doubt, the events which have occurred have speeded up the process: these events have given impetus toward its best solution and have clarified it to the large masses of Communists and workers with progressive views, and this is a positive thing. . . .

The
East European Crisis

DOCUMENT 14

*Open Letter from the Central Committee
of the Polish United Workers' Party to the
Hungarian Workers' Party,
October 28, 1956.*

To THE FIRST Secretary of the Central Committee of the HWP, Comrade Janos Kadar;

To the Premier of the Government of National Unity of Hungary, Comrade Imre Nagy:

The Central Committee of our Party, our entire Party, and the entire Polish nation are listening with the greatest pain and deep disquiet to the tragic news coming from your country. We are shocked by the shedding of fraternal blood and by the conflagration which are destroying your capital. This is why we ask you to transmit to our Hungarian brothers— members of the HWP, the entire Hungarian working class, the entire Hungarian people, so cordially close to us—the following appeal.

From Paul E. Zinner, ed., *National Communism and Popular Revolt in Eastern Europe: A Selection of Documents on Events in Poland and Hungary February-November, 1956* (New York: Columbia University Press, 1956), pp. 444-45. Reprinted by permission of the publisher. A similar letter from the Yugoslav party, dated October 28, 1956, appears in the same volume, pp. 446-48.

Brother Hungarians!

In these tragic days for you, we hold that we must not remain silent. For centuries our nations have been linked by a common love of liberty. We fought for it, shoulder to shoulder, in the last century against the aggressive monarchs. We fought for it, twelve years ago, against Hitlerite fascism, against the native landlords, and factory owners. And even in the past few days we took up—you and we—simultaneously and in solidarity, the struggle for socialist democratization of our countries, for equality and sovereignty in relations between socialist countries.

All this gives us the right to turn to you with an ardent appeal.

Brother Hungarians!

Stop the shedding of fraternal blood!

We know the program of the Government of National Unity of Hungary, the program of socialist democracy, of betterment of living standards, of creation of workers' councils, of full national sovereignty, of the withdrawal of Soviet troops from Hungary, of the basing of friendship with the Soviet Union on the Leninist principles of equality.

We are far from interfering in your internal affairs. We judge, however, that this program corresponds to the interests of the Hungarian people, and of the entire camp of peace. It seems to us that all Hungarian patriots, including those who are today on the other side of the barricade, can agree with this program.

We think that only those who wish to turn Hungary back from the road to socialism could reject the program of the Government of National Unity of Hungary.

We appeal especially ardently to the Hungarian working class on which rests the chief responsibility for the fate of the country to defend the people's authority and socialism, to defend the unity of the camp of socialism, dear to you and to us, [based] on principles of equality and sovereignty of all countries.

Brother Hungarians!

You and we are on the same side, the side of freedom and socialism. We call to you: enough blood, enough destruction, enough fratricidal struggle. May peace come to reign in Hungary, peace and unity of the nation so indispensable for the realization of the broad program of democratization, progress, and socialism which has been put forward by your Government of National Unity.

The Central Committee of the
Polish United Workers Party

DOCUMENT 15

Declaration by the Soviet Government on
"Principles of Development and Further
Strengthening of Friendship and
Cooperation Between the Soviet Union and
Other Socialist States," October 30, 1956.

THE POLICY OF peaceful coexistence, friendship, and cooperation among all countries was and remains the immutable basis of the foreign relations of the Union of Soviet Socialist Republics. This policy finds its most profound and consistent expression in the relations between the socialist countries. United as they are by the common ideal of building a socialist society and by the principles of proletarian internationalism, the countries of this great commonwealth of socialist nations can build their relations with one another only on a basis of full equality, respect for each other's territorial integrity, independence and sovereignty, and non-interference in each other's internal affairs. This does not preclude, but on the contrary, presupposes close fraternal cooperation and mutual assistance in the economic, political and cultural fields.

It was on this basis that the system of people's democracy arose, gained strength and displayed its great virility in several European and Asian countries after the second world war and the defeat of fascism. The process of establishing the new system and implementing far-reaching revolutionary reforms of social relationships was attended by no small number of difficulties, unsolved problems and outright mistakes, which extended also to relations between the socialist countries. These violations and mistakes tended to deprecate the principle of equality in relations between the socialist countries.

The Twentieth Congress of the Communist Party of the Soviet Union resolutely condemned these violations and mistakes and declared that it would be the task of the Soviet Union consistently to apply its Leninist principles of equality of nations in its relations with other socialist countries. The Twentieth Congress declared that full account must be taken of the historical past and specific features of each country that has taken the path of building the new life. . . .

The Soviet government is prepared to discuss with the governments of

From *New Times,* no. 45, 1956.

the other socialist countries measures to ensure the further development and strengthening of economic contacts between socialist countries, with a view to eliminating any possibility whatever of violation of the principle of national sovereignty, mutual benefit and equality in economic relations.

That principle must be applied also to advisers. In the early period, when the new social system was taking shape, the Soviet Union, at the request of the governments of the People's Democracies, dispatched a number of its experts to these countries—engineers, agronomists, scientific workers, military advisers. In the recent period the Soviet government has on several occasions raised with the socialist countries the question of recalling its advisers.

In view of the fact that the People's Democracies have developed their own competent personnel in all branches of economic and military endeavour, the Soviet government considers it urgent to discuss with the other socialist countries whether it is advisable to retain the Soviet advisers there. . . .

With a view to ensuring the mutual security of the socialist countries, the Soviet government is prepared to examine with the other socialist countries signatory to the Warsaw Treaty the question of Soviet troops stationed in the territory of the above-mentioned countries. In this the Soviet government proceeds from the general principle that the troops of any Warsaw Power may be stationed in the territory of another Warsaw Power by agreement of all the Treaty members, and solely with the consent of the country in whose territory the troops have been stationed at its request, or are proposed to be stationed.

The Soviet government considers it necessary to make a statement in connection with the events in Hungary. The development of these events has shown that the working people of Hungary, which has made big progress on the basis of the people's-democratic system, have rightly raised the question of the need to eliminate the serious shortcomings in economic development, further improve the material well-being of the population and combat bureaucratic distortions in the government apparatus. However, the dark forces of reaction and counter-revolution attached themselves to this just and progressive movement of the working people and are attempting to utilize the discontent of part of the working population to undermine the foundations of the people's democratic system in Hungary and re-establish landlord and capitalist rule.

The Soviet government, like the entire Soviet people, deeply regrets that the development of events in Hungary has led to bloodshed.

At the request of the Hungarian people's government, the Soviet government agreed to bring Soviet military units into Budapest in order to help the Hungarian People's Army and the Hungarian authorities to establish order in the city.

In view of the fact that the continued presence of Soviet military units in Hungary may serve as a pretext for still further aggravation of the situation, the Soviet government has ordered its military command to withdraw the Soviet units from Budapest as soon as the Hungarian government considers this necessary.

At the same time, the Soviet Government is prepared to begin negotiations with the government of the Hungarian People's Republic and other parties to the Warsaw Treaty on the question of Soviet troops in Hungarian territory.

It is now the chief and sacred duty of all workers, peasants, intellectual, of all the Hungarian working people, to defend the socialist gains of their People's Democracy. . . .

DOCUMENT 16

Communiqué on Talks Between Soviet
and Polish Communist Party and State
Leaders, Moscow, November 18, 1956.

THE MEETINGS AND negotiations, held in an atmosphere of cordiality and friendship and in a spirit of mutual understanding and frankness, provided an opportunity for a fruitful exchange of opinions on questions relating to the development and strengthening of the mutual relations between the Soviet Union and the Polish People's Republic, and on major international problems.

The negotiations and the exchange of opinions between the delegations revealed a mutual desire to base relations between the Communist Party of the Soviet Union and the Polish United Worker's Party, and between our two countries, on the Leninist principles of equality of nations, and showed that the U.S.S.R. and P.P.R. hold similar views on the major international problems of the day. . . .

The delegations exchanged opinions on the events in Hungary. They expressed the confidence that the Hungarian working class and the whole Hungarian people will be able to uphold the achievements of the people's

From *New Times*, no. 45, 1956.

democratic system. The U.S.S.R. and Poland will support the Revolutionary Workers' and Peasants' Government [the Kadar regime, installed by Soviet arms—ED.] whose program disavows the pernicious errors which marked the policy of the former Rakosi government and aims at developing socialist democracy and promoting fraternal cooperation with other socialist countries on the basis of the full equality and respect of sovereignty. The delegations believe that the purpose of certain United Nations decisions on Hungary is not to assist the Hungarian people, but to divert the attention of the peoples from the aggression against Egypt.

In the course of their friendly negotiations, the delegations thoroughly examined and discussed every aspect of the present state of relations between the Soviet Union and Poland.

The parties believe that the Soviet Government's Declaration of October 30, 1956, [see Document 15—ED.] on the principles for further strengthening friendship and cooperation between the Soviet Union and other socialist countries is of great importance for the development and consolidation of friendship between the socialist countries. They believe that the principles set forth in this Declaration accord with the decisions passed on these questions by the Eighth Plenary Session of the Central Committee of the Polish United Workers' Party [which ushered in the Gomulka government and its insistence on increased independence—ED.] and with the policy of the Polish government. In the course of the present negotiations the parties devoted special attention to the further development and strengthening of friendship between the peoples of the Soviet Union and the Polish People's Republic, and expressed their confidence that the indestructible alliance and fraternal friendship between the two countries will continue to grow in strength and scope, in keeping with the principles of full equality, respect for territorial integrity, independence and sovereignty, and non-interference in internal affairs. . . .

The parties discussed questions connected with the temporary stationing of Soviet military units on Polish territory.

They established that it has not yet been possible to reach agreed decisions that would give the European countries sufficient guarantees against the revival of German militarism. The fact that the validity of existing international boundaries in Europe, and primarily of the established and existing Western boundary of Poland, is being constantly challenged by the revanchist forces is another serious factor hampering normalization of relations in Europe.

The parties came to the conclusion that, in view of this state of affairs, and also of the present international situation, the temporary stationing of Soviet troops on Polish territory is still advisable, and this moreover owing to the necessity of retaining Soviet troops in Germany on the basis of international treaties and agreements.

It was agreed that the parties will consult with each other on the question of the retention of Soviet military units on Polish territory, and on their number and composition, depending on the course of international developments.

The parties also recognized the following principles defining the status of these units on Polish territory:

the temporary presence of Soviet troops in Poland shall in no way infringe on the sovereignty of the Polish state, nor lead to their interference in the internal affairs of the Polish People's Republic;

the location and strength of the Soviet troops shall be defined by special agreements between the parties;

the movement of Soviet military units outside their stationing areas shall require the consent of the government of the Polish People's Republic, or of other competent Polish authorities;

Soviet military units stationed on the territory of the Polish People's Republic, their personnel and the latter's families, shall be required to respect and observe the provisions of Polish law. The limits of Polish and Soviet jurisdiction with regard to Soviet military personnel in Poland shall be established by special agreement;

times and routes of, and the procedures for, the transit of Soviet troops through the territory of the Polish People's Republic shall be established by agreement of the parties.

An appropriate agreement defining the legal status of Soviet troops during their temporary stationing on Polish territory shall be concluded within the near future. . . .*

[Signed by Khrushchev, Bulganin, Gomulka, and Cyrankiewicz.]

* A treaty on this matter was signed in Warsaw, December 17, 196 (translated in *The Current Digest of the Soviet Press,* VIII, no. 51, pp. 3-5).

DOCUMENT 17

*"Joint Statement of the Governments of the
Chinese People's Republic and the
Polish People's Republic," April 11, 1957.*

. . . THE SOCIALIST COUNTRIES are linked by the common goal of struggle
for the construction of socialist and communist society. The socialist countries are guided by the common ideas of Marxism-Leninism. These common
ideas and this goal firmly bind together the Soviet Union, Poland, China,
and the other socialist countries. Both sides are full of determination to do
all in their power for the further strenghtening of the unity of the camp of
socialism on the basis of the Marxist-Leninist principles of proletarian internationalism and the equality of rights of nations.

Both sides note with satisfaction that there has recently been a series of
negotiations among socialist countries on the basis of the principles of
the equality of rights of nations, mutual respect for sovereignty, noninterference in the internal affairs of one another, equality and mutual benefit,
which have led to the further improvement and strengthening of the unity
and friendly relations among them. Both sides express satisfaction in the
results that have been achieved thanks to this reenforcement of the socialist
countries.

Both sides consider that the construction of socialism in accord with the
teachings of Marxism-Leninism represents the highest interests of the peoples of both countries, that in the course of the construction of socialism
in each of the two countries, taking account of the special national peculiarities and the concrete conditions, it is consequently necessary to struggle
against any deviations and to oppose both dogmatism and revisionism.
Herein lies the reliable guarantee of the effective surmounting of difficulties
and the undercutting of all the designs of inimical forces that are directed
toward undermining socialist construction.

Both sides again affirm [having previously done so in a statement of
January 16, 1957—ED.] that they support the Revolutionary Worker-
Peasant government of the Hungarian People's Republic in its struggle for
the consolidation of the socialist order and the liquidation of the consequences of past errors and will continue to render aid to the Hungarian
people in overcoming difficulties, which they face at the present time.

The Chinese Peoples' Republic notes with pleasure the successes achieved
by the Polish United Workers' Party since the Eighth Plenum of its Central

From *Izvestiia*, April 12, 1957. Editor's translation.

Committee [which ousted the Stalinists and installed Gomulka in October, 1956—ED.] All the popular-democratic forces in Poland are with each day more firmly rallying around the Central Committee of the Polish United Workers' Party headed by Comrade Gomulka. . . . The government of the Chinese Peoples' Republic is profoundly convinced that the Polish Peoples' Republic will make still more important contributions to the cause of strengthening the great commonwealth of socialist countries.

Both sides note with satisfaction that with each day the relations of co-operation between the Chinese Peoples' Republic and the Polish Peoples' Republic are strengthening and developing in the spirit of fraternity in the fields of politics, economics, shipping and culture. . . .

Both sides declare that the governments of both countries will further develop friendship and cooperation between the two countries in the fields mentioned, that in case of need they will consult with one another, guided by the spirit of mutual understanding and fraternal cooperation, on important questions raised by the interests of both countries. . . .

[Signed by Chou En-lai and J. Cyrankiewicz.]

Antirevisionism
and the Quest for Unity

DOCUMENT 18

"Declaration of the Conference of Representatives of Communist and Workers' Parties of Socialist Countries," Moscow, November 22, 1957.

REPRESENTATIVES OF THE . . . [Albanian, Bulgarian, Hungarian, Vietnamese, East German, Chinese, Korean, Mongolian, Polish, Rumanian,

From *Soviet News,* November 22, 1957.

Soviet, and Czechoslovak parties—and also the Yugoslav Communist Party, which alone did not sign this document—ED.] discussed their relations, current problems of the international situation and the struggle for peace and socialism.

The exchange of opinions revealed identity of views of the parties on all the questions examined at the meeting and unanimity in their assessment of the international situation. In the course of discussion the meeting also touched upon general problems of the international Communist movement. In drafting the declaration the participants in the meeting consulted with representatives of the fraternal parties in the capitalist countries. The fraternal parties not present at this meeting will assess and themselves decide what action they should take on the considerations expressed in the declaration.

1. The main content of our epoch is the transition from capitalism to socialism which was begun by the great October socialist revolution in Russia. Today more than a third of the population of the world—over 950 million people—have taken the road of socialism and are building a new life. . . .

2. The meeting considers that in the present situation the strengthening of the unity and fraternal cooperation of the socialist countries, the Communist and Workers' Parties and the solidarity of the international working-class, national liberation, and democratic movements acquire special significance.

At bedrock of the relations of the world socialist system and all the Communist and Workers' Parties lie the principles of Marxism-Leninism, the principles of proletarian internationalism which have been tested by life. Today the vital interests of the working people of all countries call for their support of the Soviet Union and all the socialist countries who, pursuing a policy of preserving peace throughout the world, are the mainstay of peace and social progress. The working class, the democratic forces and the working people everywhere are interested in tirelessly strengthening fraternal contacts for the sake of the common cause, in safeguarding from enemy encroachments the historical, political and social gains effected in the Soviet Union—the first and mightiest social power—in the Chinese People's Republic and in all the socialist countries, in seeing these gains extended and consolidated.

The socialist countries base their relations on principles of complete equality, respect for territorial integrity, state independence, and sovereignty and non-interference in one another's affairs. These are vital principles. However, they do not exhaust the essence of relations between them. Fraternal mutual aid is part and parcel of these relations. This aid is a striking expression of socialist internationalism. . . .

3. . . . Of vital importance in the present stage is intensified struggle against opportunist trends in the working class and communist movement. The meeting underlines the necessity of resolutely overcoming revisionism and dogmatism in the ranks of the Communist and Workers' Parties. Revisionism and dogmatism in the working class and communist movement are today, as they have been in the past, international phenomena. Dogmatism and sectarianism hinder the development of Marxist-Leninist theory and its creative application in the changing conditions, replace the study of the concrete situation with merely quoting classics and sticking to books, and leads to the isolation of the party from the masses. A party that has withdrawn into the shell of sectarianism and that has lost contact with the masses cannot bring victory to the cause of the working class.

In condemning dogmatism, the Communist Parties believe that the main danger at present is revisionism or, in other words, right-wing opportunism, which as a manifestation of bourgeois ideology paralyses the revolutionary energy of the working class and demands the preservation or restoration of capitalism. However, dogmatism and sectarianism can also be the main danger at different phases of development in one party or another. It is for each Communist Party to decide what danger threatens it more at a given time. . . .

4. The communist and workers' parties are faced with great historic tasks. The carrying out of these tasks necessitates closer unity not only of the communist and workers' parties, but of the entire working class, necessitates cementing the alliance of the working class and peasantry, rallying the working people and progressive mankind, the freedom and peace-loving forces of the world.

The defense of peace is the most important world-wide task of the day. The communist and workers' parties in all countries stand for joint action on the broadest possible scale with all forces favoring peace and opposed to war. The participants in the meeting declare that they support the efforts of all states, parties, organizations, movements, and individuals who champion peace and oppose war, who want peaceful co-existence, collective security in Europe and Asia, reduction of armaments, and prohibition of the use and tests of nuclear weapons. . . .

The forms of the transition of socialism may vary for different countries. The working class and its vanguard—the Marxist-Leninist Party—seek to achieve the socialist revolution by peaceful means. This would accord with the interests of the working class and the people as a whole as well as with the national interests of the country. . . .

In the event of the ruling classes resorting to violence against people, the possibility of non-peaceful transition to socialism should be borne in mind. Leninism teaches, and experience confirms, that the ruling classes never relinquish power voluntarily. In this case the degree of bitterness and the forms of the class struggle will depend not so much on the proletariat as on the resistance put up by the reactionary circles to the will of the overwhelming majority of the people, on these circles using force at one or another stage of the struggle for socialism.

The possibility of one or another way to socialism depends on the concrete conditions in each country. . . .

Contrary to the absurd assertions of imperialism about a so-called crisis of communism, the Communist movement is growing and gathering strength. The historic decisions of the 20th Congress of the CPSU are of tremendous importance not only to the CPSU and to the building of Communism in the U.S.S.R., they have opened a new stage in the world Communist movement and pushed ahead its further development along Marxist-Leninist lines. The results of the Congresses of the Communist Parties of China, France, Italy and other countries in recent times have clearly demonstrated the unity and solidarity of the party ranks and their loyalty to the principles of proletarian internationalism. This meeting of the representatives of Communist and Workers' Parties testifies to the international solidarity of the Communist movement.

After exchanging views, the participants in the meeting arrived at the conclusion that in present conditions it is expedient besides bilateral meetings of leading personnel and exchange of information, to hold, as the need arises, more representative conferences of Communist and Workers' Parties to discuss current problems, share experience, study each other's views and attitudes and concert action in the joint struggle for the common goals— peace, a democracy, and socialism.

The participants in the meeting unanimously express their firm confidence that, by closing their ranks and thereby rallying the working class and the peoples of all countries, the Communist and Workers' Parties will surmount all obstacles in their onward movement and accelerate further big victories for the cause of peace, democracy, and socialism.

DOCUMENT 19

Program of the Yugoslav Communist Party,
April, 1958.

. . . THE YUGOSLAV COMMUNISTS do not question the forms of cooperation between Communist parties and other socialist and progressive movements, but they question the substance of this cooperation. They are in
favor of both bilateral and multilateral cooperation, on condition that it is
always based on full equality, that neither side attempts to impose its attitudes on the other, and that there is no interference in the internal relations of the parties involved. Furthermore, this cooperation must be conducive to the interests of peace, of socialism, and social progress generally.
The League of Communists of Yugoslavia considers that both bilateral
and multilateral forms of cooperation are essential elements in establishing
the unity of the activities of the socialist forces and of the progressive efforts
of mankind. If the League of Communists of Yugoslavia, under present
conditions, attributes significance primarily to various forms of bilateral
cooperation, this is because of the aforementioned objective conditions of
contemporary socialist development, and because the earlier forms of
multilateral cooperation between the workers' parties produced, besides
their positive aspects (when such forms corresponded to a definite historical
period), also negative phenomena which inflicted considerable harm on the
struggle for socialism and peace, and which the workers' movement must
overcome if it does not wish the democratic principles of socialist internationalism to be sullied once again.

Most notable among these phenomena are tendencies toward ideological
monopoly and political hegemony. Tendencies toward ideological monopoly have always been an obstacle to the development of socialist thought,
and a source of dogmatism and opportunist-revisionist reaction. And such
tendencies gave rise to the striving for an unconditional leading role in the
workers' movement, which had many negative consequences at a time when
there was not a single working class party in power. Tendencies toward
ideological monopoly can inflict even greater damage once working class
parties have come to power. The task of the workers' movement—and
especially of the Communists of the larger, more powerful and more re-

From Benes, Vaclav, Robert F. Byrnes, and Nicholas Spulber, eds., *The Second
Soviet-Yugoslav Dispute: The Full Text of the Main Documents* (Bloomington:
Indiana University, Russian and East European Institute, 1959), pp. 75-77. Re-
printed by permission of the publisher.

sponsible socialist countries—is to fight, both in theory and in practice, for relations of equality. In doing so they should start from the principle that validity and the progressive nature of a given ideology, or of given forms of socialist development, depend exclusively on the vital value of that ideology in practice, and not on the approval of one or another international body. Any aspect of ideological monopoly which would hamper free socialist development in socialist countries would act as a brake on the development of international socialism generally. For this reason the League of Communists of Yugoslavia considers that only those forms of international cooperation which unite, on the widest possible basis, efforts to solve common problems of the struggle for peace, of the struggle for socialism and socialist development, are expedient at present.

The interest of further socialist development demands free socialist democratic relations between the parties of the socialist countries. In the struggle for the victory of socialism, the working class of one or another country may, for a certain period of time, be the standard-bearer of that struggle, its vanguard, or possess greater material power; but that does not entitle it to a monopoly position in the workers' movement, least of all to monopoly in the sphere of ideology. Past experience has shown, and is making it even clearer today, that cooperation in the workers' movement is possible only between equals. . . .

To proclaim the path and the form of socialist development in any single country as being the only correct path and form, is nothing but a dogma which obstructs the process of the socialist transformation of the world. The general aims of socialism are common to all, but the rate and forms of progress of society toward these aims are and must be different in keeping with the concrete conditions of different countries and different parts of the world. The freedom of internal socialist development and the absence of any attempt to impose specific forms on others, noninterference in the internal life and internal development of other movements, as well as free and equal exchange of experiences and socialist theoretical thought, should be the fundamental principle of the mutual relations between socialist countries and socialist movements.

Attempts at branding recognition of the diversity of forms in socialist processes as a "new" ideological phenomenon, as the birth of "National Communism," have no connection whatever with the scientific explanation of contemporary socialist development. Such theories can only be conceived in the minds of dogmatists, or are deliberately circulated by the representatives of the bourgeoisie with the purpose of creating disorientation and ideological confusion in the workers' movement. Such intentions should not prevent the elaboration of specific trends, nor should they thwart the orientation of the working class towards the problems and conditions of their own country. . . .

DOCUMENT 20

"Long Live Leninism," April 16, 1960.

APRIL 22 OF this year is the ninetieth anniversary of the birth of Lenin. . . . Under the banner of Lenin, under the banner of the October Revolution, a new world revolution began, with the proletarian revolution playing the leading role. A new era dawned in human history.

Through the October Revolution, the voice of Lenin quickly resounded throughout the world. The Chinese people's anti-imperialist, anti-feudal May 4 Movement in 1919, as Comrade Mao Tse-tung put it, "came into being at the call of the world revolution of that time, of the Russian Revolution and of Lenin."

The modern revisionists, proceeding from their absurd arguments on the current world situation and from their absurd argument that the Marxist-Leninist theory of class analysis and class struggle is obsolete, attempt to totally overthrow the fundamental theories of Marxism-Leninism on a series of questions like violence, war, peaceful coexistence, etc.

There are also some people who are not revisionists, but well-intentioned persons who sincerely want to be Marxists, but get confused in the face of certain new historical phenomena and thus have some incorrect ideas. For example, some of them say that the failure of the U.S. imperialists' policy of atomic blackmail marks the end of violence. While thoroughly refuting the absurdities of the modern revisionists, we should also help these well-intentioned people to correct their erroneous ideas. . . .

We believe in the absolute correctness of Lenin's thinking: War is an inevitable outcome of systems of exploitation and the source of modern wars is the imperialist system. Until the imperialist system and the exploiting classes come to an end, wars of one kind or another will always occur. They may be wars among the imperialists for redivision of the world, or wars of aggression and anti-aggression between the imperialists and the oppressed nations, or civil wars of revolution and counter-revolution between the exploited and exploiting classes in the imperialist countries, or, of course, wars

From *Peking Review*, no. 17, 1960. The authorship of the article is given as "the editorial departments of *Jen-min Jih-pao and Hung-chi*."

in which the imperialists attack the socialist countries and the socialist countries are forced to defend themselves. All these kinds of wars represent the
continuation of the policies of definite classes. Marxists-Leninists absolutely
must not sink into the mire of bourgeois pacifism, and can only appraise all
these kinds of wars and thus draw conclusions for proletarian policy by
adopting the method of concrete class analysis. As Lenin put it: "Theoret-
ically, it would be quite wrong to forget that every war is but the continuation of politics by other means." . . .

Modern revisionists seek to confuse the peaceful foreign policy of the
socialist countries with the domestic policies of the proletariat in the capitalist countries. They thus hold that peaceful co-existence of countries with
differing social systems means that capitalism can peacefully grow into socialism, that the proletariat in countries ruled by the bourgeoisie can re-
nounce class struggle and enter into "peaceful cooperation" with the bourgeoisie and the imperialists, and that the proletariat and all the exploited
classes should forget about the fact that they are living in a class society,
and so on. All these views are also diametrically opposed to Marxism-
Leninism. They are put forward in an attempt to protect imperialist rule
and hold the proletariat and all the rest of the working people perpetually
in capitalist enslavement.

Peaceful co-existence of nations and people's revolutions in various countries are in themselves two different things, not one and the same thing; two
different concepts, not one; two different kinds of question, and not one and
the same kind of question.

Peaceful co-existence refers to relations between nations; revolution
means the overthrow of the oppressors as a class by the oppressed people
within each country, while in the case of the colonial and semi-colonial
countries, it is first and foremost a question of overthrowing alien oppressors,
namely, the imperialists. Before the October Revolution the question of
peaceful co-existence between socialist and capitalist countries simply did
not exist in the world, as there were as yet no socialist countries; but there
did exist at that time the questions of the proletarian revolution and the
national revolution, as the peoples in various countries, in accordance with
their own specific conditions, had long ago put revolutions of one kind or
the other on the agenda of the day to determine the destinies of their countries. . . .

Are the teachings of Marxism-Leninism now "outmoded"? Does the
whole, integrated teaching of Lenin on imperialism, on proletarian revolution and proletarian dictatorship, on war and peace, and on the building of
socialism and communism still retain its vigorous vitality? If it is still valid
and does retain vigorous vitality, does this refer only to a certain por-

tion of it or to the whole? We usually say that Leninism is Marxism in the epoch of imperialism and proletarian revolution, Marxism in the epoch of the victory of socialism and communism. Does this view remain correct? Can it be said that Lenin's original conclusions and our usual conception of Leninism have lost their validity and correctness, and that therefore we should turn back and accept those revisionist and opportunist conclusions which Lenin long ago smashed to smithereens and which have gone disgracefully bankrupt in actual life? These questions now confront us and must be answered. Marxist-Leninists must thoroughly expose the absurdities of the imperialists and modern revisionists on these questions, eradicate their influence among the masses, awaken those they have temporarily hoodwinked and further arouse the revolutionary will of the masses.

Document 21

Khrushchev's Speech to the Conference of Communist Party Representatives, Bucharest, June 21, 1960.

We do not intend to yield to [American] provocations and to deviate from the general line of our foreign policy, which was laid down by the 20th CPSU Congress and approved in the Declaration of the Communist and Workers' Parties, adopted in 1957, during the celebrations of the 40th anniversary of the Great October Socialist Revolution.

This is a policy of co-existence, a policy of consolidating peace, easing international tension and doing away with the cold war.

The thesis that in our time war is not inevitable has a direct bearing on the policy of peaceful co-existence proclaimed at the 20th and 21st Congresses of our party. Lenin's propositions about imperialism remain in force and are still a lodestar for us in our theory and practice. But it should not be forgotten that Lenin's propositions on imperialism were advanced and developed tens of years ago, when the world did not know many things that are now decisive for historical development, for the entire international situation.

Some of Lenin's propositions on imperialism date back to the period when there was no Soviet Union, when the other socialist countries did not exist.

From *Soviet News*, June 22, 1960.

The powerful Soviet Union, with its enormous economic and military potential, is now growing and gaining in strength; the great socialist camp, which now numbers over 1,000 million people, is growing and gaining in strength; the organization and political consciousness of the working class have grown, and even in the capitalist countries it is actively fighting for peace. Such factors are in operation now as, for instance, the broad movement of peace champions; the number of countries coming out for peace among nations is increasing. It should also be pointed out that imperialism no longer has such a rear to fall back upon as the colonial system which it had formerly.

Besides, comrades, one cannot mechanically repeat now on this question what Vladimir Ilyich Lenin said many decades ago on imperialism, and go on asserting that imperialist wars are inevitable until socialism triumphs throughout the world. We are now living in such a period when the forces of socialism are increasingly growing and becoming stronger, where ever-broader masses of the working people are rallying behind the banner of Marxism-Leninism.

History will possibly witness such a time when capitalism is preserved only in a small number of states, maybe states for instance, as small as a button on a coat. Well? And even in such conditions would one have to look up in a book what Vladimir Ilyich Lenin quite correctly said for his time, would one just have to repeat that wars are inevitable since capitalist countries exist?

Of course, the essence of capitalism, of imperialism, does not change even if it is represented by small countries. It is common knowledge that a wolf is just as bloodthirsty a beast of prey as a lion or a tiger, although he is much weaker. That is why man fears less to meet a wolf than a tiger or a lion. Of course, small beasts of prey can also bite, essentially they are the same but they have different possibilities, they are not so strong and it is easier to render them harmless.

Therefore one cannot ignore the specific situation, the changes in the correlation of forces in the world and repeat what the great Lenin said in quite different historical conditions. If Lenin could rise from his grave he would take such people, as one says, to task and would teach them how one must understand the essence of the matter.

We live in a time when we have neither Marx, nor Engels, nor Lenin with us. If we act like children who, studying the alphabet, compile words from letters, we shall not go very far. Marx, Engels and Lenin created their immortal works which will not fade away in centuries. They indicated to mankind the road to Communism. And we confidently follow this road. On the basis of the teaching of Marxism-Leninism we must think ourselves, profoundly study life, analyze the present situation and draw the conclusions which benefit the common cause of Communism.

One must not only be able to read but also correctly understand what one has read and apply it in the specific conditions of the time in which we live, taking into consideration the existing situation, and the real balance of forces. A political leader acting in this manner shows that he not only can read but can also creatively apply the revolutionary teaching. If he does not do this, he resembles a man about whom people say: "He looks into a book, but sees nothing!"

All this gives grounds for saying with confidence that under present conditions war is not inevitable.

He who fails to understand this does not believe in the strength and creative abilities of the working class, underestimates the power of the socialist camp, does not believe in the great force of attraction of socialism, which has demonstrated its superiority over capitalism with the utmost clarity.

Is the possibility of the imperialists unleashing war under present conditions ruled out? We have said several times and we repeat once again: No, it is not. But the imperialist countries cannot fail to take into account the power of the Soviet Union, the power of the socialist camp as a whole. Naturally, the imperialists do not want to trigger off war in order to perish in it. They would like to destroy the socialist countries. Therefore today even the stupid, frenzied representatives of the imperialist circles will think twice about our power before they start a military gamble. . . .

DOCUMENT 22

*"Statement of Representatives of Communist
and Workers' Parties," Moscow,
December 6, 1960.*

REPRESENTATIVES OF THE Communist and Workers' Parties have discussed at this Meeting urgent problems of the present international situation and of the further struggle for peace, national independence, democracy, and socialism.

The Meeting has shown unity of views among the participants on the issues discussed. The Communist and Workers' Parties have unanimously re-

From *World Marxist Review,* no. 12, 1960.

affirmed their allegiance to the Declaration and Peace Manifesto adopted in 1957. These program documents of creative Marxism-Leninism determined the fundamental positions of the international Communist movement on the more important issues of our time and contributed in great measure toward uniting the efforts of the Communist and Workers' Parties in the struggle to achieve common goals. They remain the banner and guide to action for the whole of the international Communist movement. . . .

A new stage has begun in the development of the world socialist system. The Soviet Union is successfully carrying on the full-scale construction of a communist society. Other countries of the socialist camp are successfully laying the foundations of socialism, and some of them have already entered the period of construction of a developed socialist society. . . .

The experience of development of the socialist countries is added evidence that mutual assistance and support, and uitilization of all the advantages of unity and solidarity among the countries of the socialist camp, are a primary international condition for their achievements and successes. Imperialist, renegade, and revisionist hopes of a split within the socialist camp are built on sand and doomed to failure. All the socialist countries cherish the unity of the socialist camp like the apple of their eye. . . .

The Declaration of 1957 points out quite correctly that undue emphasis on the role of national peculiarities and departure from the universal truth of Marxism-Leninism regarding the socialist revolution and socialist construction prejudice the common cause of socialism. The Declaration also states quite correctly that Marxism-Leninism demands creative application of the general principles of socialist revolution and socialist construction depending on the specific historical conditions in the country concerned, and does not permit of a mechanical copying of the policies and tactics of the Communist Parties of other countries. Disregard of national peculiarities may lead to the party of the proletariat being isolated from reality, from the masses, and may injure the socialist cause.

Manifestations of nationalism and national narrow-mindedness do not disappear automatically with the establishment of the socialist system. If fraternal relations and friendship between the socialist countries are to be strengthened, it is necessary that the Communist and Workers' Parties pursue a Marxist-Leninist internationalist policy, that all working people be educated in a spirit of internationalism and patriotism, and that a resolute struggle be waged to eliminate the survivals of bourgeois nationalism and chauvinism. . . .

The Communist Parties regard the fight for peace as their prime task. They call on the working class, trade unions, cooperatives, women's, and youth leagues and organizations, on all working people, irrespective of their political and religious convictions, firmly to repulse by mass struggles all acts of aggression on the part of the imperialists.

But should the imperialist maniacs start war, the people will sweep capitalism out of existence and bury it.

The foreign policy of the socialist countries rests on the firm foundation of the Leninist principle of peaceful coexistence and economic competition between the socialist and capitalist countries. In conditions of peace, the socialist system increasingly reveals its advantages over the capitalist system in all fields of economy, culture, science, and technology. The near future will bring the forces of peace and socialism new successes. The U.S.S.R. will become the leading industrial power of the world. China will become a mighty industrial state. The socialist system will be turning out more than half the world industrial product. The peace zone will expand. The working-class movement in the capitalist countries and the national-liberation movement in the colonies and dependencies will achieve new victories. The disintegration of the colonial system will become completed. The superiority of the forces of socialism and peace will be absolute. *In these conditions a real possibility will have arisen to exclude world war from the life of society even before socialism achieves complete victory on earth, with capitalism still existing in a part of the world.* The victory of socialism all over the world will completely remove the social and national causes of wars. . . .

The complete collapse of colonialism is imminent. The breakdown of the system of colonial slavery under the impact of the national-liberation movement is a development ranking second in historic importance only to the formation of the world socialist system.

The great October Socialist Revolution aroused the East and drew the colonial peoples into the common current of the world-wide revolutionary movement. This development was greatly facilitated by the Soviet Union's victory in the Second World War, the establishment of people's democracy in a number of European and Asian countries, the triumph of the socialist revolution in China, and the formation of the world socialist system. The forces of world socialism contributed decisively to the struggle of the colonial and dependent peoples for liberation from imperialist oppression. The socialist system has become a reliable shield for the independent national development of the peoples who have won freedom. The national-liberation movement receives powerful support from the international working-class movement. . . .

There are now Communist Parties active in 87 countries of the world. Their total membership exceeds 36,000,000. This is a signal victory for

Marxism-Leninism and a tremendous achievement of the working class. Like-minded Marxists are rallying in the countries which have shaken off colonial tyranny and taken the path of independent development. Communist Parties consider it their internationalist duty to promote friendship and solidarity between the working class of their countries and the working-class movement of the countries which have won their freedom in the common struggle against imperialism. . . .

The Communist Parties have unanimously condemned the Yugoslav variety of international opportunism, a variety of modern revisionist "theories" in concentrated form. After betraying Marxism-Leninism, which they termed obsolete, the leaders of the League of Communists of Yugoslavia opposed their anti-Leninist revisionist program to the Declaration of 1957; they set the YLC against the international Communist movement as a whole, severed their country from the socialist camp, made it dependent on so-called "aid" from U.S. and other imperialists, and thereby exposed the Yugoslav people to the danger of losing the revolutionary gains achieved through a heroic struggle. The Yugoslav revisionists carry on subversive work against the socialist camp and the world Communist movement. Under the pretext of being outside blocs, they engage in activities which prejudice the unity of all the peace-loving forces and countries. Further exposure of the leaders of Yugoslav revisionists and active struggle to safeguard the Communist movement and the working-class movement from the anti-Leninist ideas of the Yugoslav revisionists, remain an essential task of the Marxist-Leninist Parties. . . .

The further development of the Communist and working-class movement calls as stated in the Moscow Declaration of 1957, for continuing a determined struggle on two fronts—against revisionism, which remains the main danger, and against dogmatism and sectarianism. . . .

All the Marxist-Leninist Parties are independent and have equal rights; they shape their policies according to the specific conditions in their respective countries and in keeping with Marxist-Leninist principles, and support each other. The success of the working-class cause in any country is unthinkable without the internationalist solidarity of all Marxist-Leninist parties. Every party is responsible to the working class, to the working people of its country, to the international working-class and Communist movement as a whole.

The Communist and Workers' Parties hold meetings whenever necessary to discuss urgent problems, to share experiences, acquaint themselves with each other's views and positions, work out common views through consultations, and coordinate joint actions in the struggle for common goals.

Whenever a Party wants to clear up questions relating to the activities of another fraternal Party, its leadership approaches the leadership of the Party concerned; if necessary, they hold meetings and consultations.

The experience and results of the meetings of representatives of the Communist Parties held in recent years, particularly the results of the two major meetings—that of November 1957 and this Meeting—show that in present-day conditions such meetings are an effective form of exchanging views and experience, enriching Marxist-Leninist theory by collective effort and elaborating a common attitude in the struggle for common objectives.

The Communist and Workers' Parties unanimously declare that the Communist Party of the Soviet Union has been, and remains, the universally recognized vanguard of the world Communist movement, being the most experienced and steeled contingent of the international Communist movement. The experience which the CPSU has gained in the struggle for the victory of the working class, in socialist construction, and in the full-scale construction of communism, is of fundamental significance for the whole of the world Communist movement. The example of the CPSU and its fraternal solidarity inspire all the Communist Parties in their struggle for peace and socialism, and represent the revolutionary principles of proletarian internationalism applied in practice. The historic decisions of the 20th Congress of the CPSU are not only of great importance for the CPSU and communist construction in the U.S.S.R., but have initiated a new stage in the world Communist movement, and have promoted its development on the basis of Marxism-Leninism.

All Communist and Workers' Parties contribute to the development of the great theory of Marxism-Leninism. Mutual assistance and support in relations between all the fraternal Marxist-Leninist Parties embody the revolutionary principles of proletarian internationalism applied in practice. . . .

The meeting sees the further consolidation of the Communist Parties on the basis of Marxism-Leninism, of proletarian internationalism, as a primary condition for the unification of all working-class, democratic, and progressive forces, as a guarantee of new victories in the great struggle waged by the world Communist and working-class movement for a happy future for the whole of mankind, for the triumph of the cause of peace and socialism.

RIFT

AND

STALEMATE, 1961–1966

The signing of the "Statement" of 81 parties in 1960 ushered in not a period of unprecedented unity among Communists but rather a time of increasing antagonism between the two great powers and of self-seeking among the lesser ones. The Sino-Soviet conflict overshadowed all international relations among Communists, touching every party and state more or less directly, but the collision of the giants also increased the margin of independence of most of the smaller states and parties, as both China and Russia bargained for the international support that they could not simply command.

In this situation even the smallest Communist country might play a major role, as is illustrated by the case of Albania, which provided a major focus of interest in 1961. Relations between Khrushchev and the Albanian leader Hoxha had already become frozen in 1960, and the isolated Albanians had expressed the convergence of their outlook with that of the Chinese. But it was only in the course of 1961 that the two great powers permitted themselves to become embroiled over this peripheral case, which could have been passed by if there had been a sincere wish for conciliation in Moscow and Peking. But instead of minimizing the Albanian problem, Khrushchev sought to make it a test of his authority over small satellites and his influence over China. When the Twenty-Second Congress of the Communist Party of the Soviet Union met in October, 1961, with Premier Chou En-lai present as leader of the Chinese guests, Khrushchev attacked the Albanian Communist leadership in terms that clearly implied an appeal for their replacement (Document 24). The conciliatory attitude of the Chinese toward the Soviet party, as evidence by a fulsome letter of greeting from Mao Tse-tung, may have emboldened Khrushchev to think that he could oblige the Chinese to stand aside, leaving the Albanians overawed. Instead, Chou En-lai demonstratively walked out on the congress, pausing long enough to place a wreath on the relatively obscure grave to which the congress had just dispatched Stalin's remains. And the Albanian leadership, whether or

not they had unconditional Chinese assurances in advance, replied angrily
to Khrushchev as to an equal in the world Communist movement (Document 23). Far from having obliged the Chinese to recognize a Soviet sphere
of influence in Eastern Europe, Khrushchev had made the Albanian affair
into a sticking-point in future Sino-Soviet relations. Each power henceforth
was to insist that the other back down on the Albanian issue as a preliminary to the resolution of other problems.

China and Albania shared harsh views of Yugoslavia, the former because
Tito stood for a "soft" attitude toward "imperialism," the latter because
Yugoslavia was a constant threat on its borders. Had Khrushchev seriously
wished to alleviate the strains with Peking (or Tirana) he could at least
have maintained the hostility to Yugoslav "revisionism" to which he had
subscribed in the statement of the 81 parties. But in 1962, shortly after the
open dispute over Albania, he deliberately chose to enter into his second
reconciliation with Tito. In contrast to his reserved attitude toward Soviet
overtures in 1955, Tito was now eager to end the rift with the U.S.S.R.
and its European allies, a rift that the Yugoslavs had not wanted at any
time. Also, the Italian and Polish Communists had believed throughout the
anti-Yugoslavia campaign of 1958-1961 that Tito at least represented a
reasonable approach to European peace and relations among Communist
parties, and that he should not be excommunicated. Khrushchev no doubt
made up his own mind on this problem, but he may well have been influenced by the patent failure of the Yugoslav "revisionist" scape-goat as a
means of unifying of the other parties under Soviet guidance. And in
his anger toward the Chinese he may have deliberately chosen reconciliation with Tito, culminating in a gala state visit in Moscow in December,
1962, as a mark of his disdain for China. One might even suggest that the
leader of the once-predominant Soviet Union had come to feel the need of
an occasion to dramatize the independence of his own policy.

While the Soviet-Yugoslav reconciliation did not lead to the full integration of Yugoslavia into the Soviet-oriented bloc in Eastern Europe (e.g.,
membership in Comecon), Khrushchev did attempt to build up the economic solidarity of the U.S.S.R., East Germany, Czechoslovakia, Hungary,
Poland, Rumania, and Bulgaria (Albania having been excluded in 1961
from participation in Comecon). This was part of a continuing campaign
that included the adoption of Comecon statutes in 1960, the adoption of
"Basic Principles of the International Socialist Division of Labor" in June,
1962 (Document 25), the creation of a Comecon Executive Committee the
following month, and the proposal in November of "a unified planning organ, empowered to compile common plans." While this kind of far-reaching
integration inevitably would have increased Soviet influence in the cooper-

ating countries, only one of them took strong exception to it—Rumania. Not previously noted for its independence of Moscow, the Communist leadership of this country was in fact nursing a number of grievances concerning past Soviet highhandedness, dating all the way back to the Comintern congress of 1920 (as the Rumanian party secretary Ceauescu revealed in 1966). Most particularly the Rumanians felt economically exploited as a result of their low industrial development, and by 1960 had undertaken a major plan for heavy industry, with Soviet assistance. But the Soviet scheme for economic integration, with its implications of national specialization and supranational authority (or a supra-Rumanian authority directed by the Soviets and some other industrialized countries), contradicted Rumanian Communist goals. As the Sino-Soviet dispute developed, the Rumanians grew increasingly bolder, first resisting the Khrushchev program for Comecon behind the closed doors of the Executive Committee in February, 1963, and then with considerable publicity in their own Central Committee in April, 1964 (Document 26). Stimulated by this exercise in independence from Russia, or looking for companionship among Communist states that were similarly on their own, the Rumanians proceeded to foster friendly party-state relations with China (posing as a mediator of the Sino-Soviet quarrel, which Rumania could hardly want to see disappear entirely), Albania, and Yugoslavia. If this combination seems incongruous, one must bear in mind that the Rumanians were depending increasingly on Western ("imperialist") economic relations, shared Tito's moderate views on this topic, and also shared with him an interest in developing a major dam on the Iron Gate (gorge) of the Danube. Khrushchev's efforts at consolidation in his Eastern European backyard were counterproductive in the case of Rumania, with dire effects for Comecon as a whole.

His adventure into the backyard of another great power, the United States, also turned out poorly for inter-Communist harmony. Although Castro had taken power in Cuba not as a Communist and only later had become a self-appointed socialist leader, his regime was accepted by all Communist parties as a member of their "commonwealth," and was given economic and military sustenance by Communist countries, especially the Soviet Union, from 1959 on. One of the attractions of a socialist Cuba was its availability as a base for Soviet intermediate-range missiles, installation of which was proceeding in 1962 while the Sino-Soviet quarrel seemed quiescent. But the crisis of October, when the United States issued an ultimatum on the removal of the missiles, helped to inflame the Sino-Soviet quarrel. At the very time Khrushchev publicly withdrew the missiles, the Chinese launched a military attack on territory they claimed along the northeast frontier of India. In this encounter the Soviets first tried to equivocate, which pleased neither China nor India, and then determined to offer to sell India military aircraft, in addition to previous deliveries. Thus from China's viewpoint, the Soviet Union was simultaneously making a corrupt deal with American imperialism and arming bourgeois India against Communist China. Her gloomiest suspicions concerning Khrushchev's ideological rectitude seemed proven.

All this no doubt provided fuel for more acrimonious relations in the future between the two great powers, but it did not create an open schism at once. One inhibition was the expressed desire of various Communist parties, including the North Vietnamese, New Zealand, Indonesian, Swedish, and British, for a general international conference of reunification. Both of the giant Communist powers were wary of such a gathering, but interested in the possibilities of using negotiations of some sort to advance their own doctrines. Had their main goal sincerely been conciliation, the Sino-Soviet correspondence of February-June, 1963, probably would have remained unpublished, as had an exchange in the first half of 1962. But both sides (especially the Chinese) evidently were so convinced of the righteous persuasiveness of the their respective cases that they were willing to publish long, programmatic letters, which clearly prejudiced the chances for bilateral discussions (Documents 27-28). It was no surprise that the secret discussions in July, 1963, between party delegations failed to advance matters toward any kind of settlement at a general conference.

Even as the Sino-Soviet party negotiations were proceeding, the Soviets showed their fundamental hostility to the Chinese, publishing a long open letter against the Chinese addressed to members of the Soviet party and opening negotiations with the American and British governments concerning a treaty ending nuclear testing in the atmosphere. The Chinese, deprived of Soviet aid in nuclear development, could not consent to such an agreement and in any case were not invited to the Moscow negotiations on this matter, which could easily be interpreted as a Soviet-American cabal. Not having been consulted by the Soviet government in this matter, the Chinese did not deign to send a diplomatic note to Moscow, instead issuing a statement condemning the treaty, to which the Soviets replied, defending it.

On November 29, 1963, Khrushchev sent a personally signed letter to the Chinese party leaders (apparently his first) in a seeming attempt to initiate a more conciliatory mood, proposing the improvement of state relations (e.g., economic ties) and the elimination of public polemics (Document 29). If this was a sincere change of heart, the Chinese did not interpret it as such and disdained to reply until after the Soviets had concluded that a severe anti-Chinese campaign among all the Communist parties was in order. The Soviet leadership seems to have prepared for this during December,

1963-January, 1964 (anticipating and perhaps hoping for the failure of the conciliatory overture). The emphasis on "splitters" in the new Soviet propaganda offensive suggests that one major consideration in the new tactic was the growing danger of Chinese proselytization among other Communist parties. As the Sino-Soviet split had gained momentum, the Chinese had been increasingly active in advertising their views through their diplomatic establishments, delegates to various international meetings, their increasing stream of publications, and their adherents in this or that country. In the case of Albania, of course, they had an outright disciple (Hoxha), and most of the south and east Asian parties, in or out of power (excepting the Soviet satellite Mongolia), were inclined to their side. Castro's Cuba, while dependent on Soviet economic support, was sympathetic to the vociferous anti-Americanism of China. And splinter groups, separating from the traditional, Moscow-oriented Communist parties, appeared in such diverse places as Belguim, Brazil, and the United States. Where this would end was hard to say, but the tendency of the Asian Communists to side with China and the possible appeal of the Chinese in all underdeveloped or non-White areas was ominous for the Soviets. Their course in February, 1964, was fixed on securing the general condemnation of the Chinese Communists by the majority of the world's Communist parties, despite the cost of a split. The campaign was opened on February 12 by a harshly anti-Chinese, confidential circular letter to most Communist parties, followed by the presentation of a major anti-Chinese resolution by the inter-Communist relations expert Suslov to a session of the central committee. The normal size of this high party body was 330, but to emphasize the importance of the occasion guests from other Soviet organizations had been invited to swell the total attending (and voting) to 6,000.

The Chinese replied to this challenge, inaugurating a correspondence of unprecedented bitterness that extended from February through August, 1964 (Documents 30-38). The gist of it and an active press campaign on both sides was that the Soviets were planning on a new world meeting, preceded by a preparatory session as in 1960, which would presumably settle matters by condemning the heretics, who declared in advance that they would not appear before such a kangaroo court. As the convocation of the preparatory meeting, scheduled for December 15, 1964, drew closer, tension increased. The Chinese were adamant, their allies (such as the Japanese party) were unmoved by Soviet pressure (Documents 39-40), and some of the parties not on the Chinese side (such as the Rumanian and Italian) were unhappy about Soviet tactics and unenthusiastic about a "victory" that would leave them in a Soviet-dominated fragment of the Communist movement (Documents 41-42).

At this juncture the world was astonished to learn that on October 14, 1964, Khrushchev had yielded up his positions of authority in the Soviet party and state. While official Soviet statements did not explicitly relate Khrushchev's downfall to errors in dealing with foreign Communists, the replacement of this central figure had repercussions on Soviet relations with both its allies and opponents among Communists. The Chinese were naturally pleased, enough so to send Chou En-lai to Moscow in honor of the November 7 anniversary of the Bolshevik revolution. But they were reserved, too, and with good reason in view of the continued presence of Suslov, who had played such a major role in Soviet policy toward China during the most acrimonious encounters of 1963-1964. Many European Communists, who had come to regard Khrushchev as a supporter of their autonomy, were dismayed. The Italian Communist Party, whose old leader Togliatti had died shortly before Khrushchev resigned, expressed open dissatisfaction with the conspiratorial way the deposition was carried out, while the new Soviet bosses, Brezhnev and Kosygin, flew to Poland to give private explanations to Gomulka concerning the affair. On balance it seems that the fall of Khrushchev undermined the confidence in Soviet leadership among foreign Communists who were favorably disposed to Soviet policies, while it did nothing of lasting importance to heal the rift with China and her followers. The new Soviet leadership backed down on the campaign to settle matters with China, dropping the whole idea of a general Communist conference and changing the scheduled preparatory meeting of December into a flaccid "consultative meeting" in March, 1965 (Document 43). The original Khrushchevian plan was that it should be attended by the same 26 parties that participated in the preliminary session of 1960, but in fact only 18 of them appeared, the missing ones being Albania, Vietnam, China, Korea, Rumania, Indonesia, Japan, and U.S.A. (although the latter sent an observer). For a year after the resignation of Khrushchev, Soviet polemics against China ceased, and were resumed in November, 1965, only in moderated form. The Chinese made it clear that they found the new Soviet leadership no improvement on Khrushchev (Document 44), even though the open, direct attack on China had been halted.

Neither side seemed able to find a fruitful tactic with which to break loose from the stalemate. The intensification of the war in Vietnam in 1965-1966 provided the Soviets with an opportunity to demonstrate their toughness against "imperialism," for they were best equipped to supply weapons, especially air defense weapons, to the North Vietnamese. While this won the Soviets some credit in North Vietnam, which consented to send a delegation to the Soviet party congress of March-April, 1966, it did not impress the Chinese, who refused to send representatives. One of their specific pretexts for this symbolic breach in interparty relations was a sharp Soviet letter that was sent to various Communist parties prior to the congress (Document 45). The most striking feature of the Sino-Soviet exchange of late 1965 and early 1966 was the indications that the war in Vietnam was aggravating the great rift in Communism.

In other areas both the Soviets and Chinese suffered setbacks to their international influence. The Soviets had been counting on the "national democracies" that they supported to evolve into Communist, Soviet-oriented regimes. For example, the Algerian leftist Ben Bella was accorded a place of honor on the Lenin mausoleum on May Day, 1964, as part of the campaign to draw his revolutionary government into the "socialist commonwealth." The Chinese had not approved of this conception of evolutionary birth for Communist regimes, and to some extent could consider their views justified by the overthrow by non-Communists of Ben Bella in Algeria in 1965 and Nkrumah in Ghana in 1966. But their influence among foreign Communists was seriously weakened by events in Indonesia and Cuba in 1965-1966. The Indonesian Communist Party, which was probably the most important one in Asia after the Chinese, whom they generally followed, was physically devastated in October, 1965, following an unsuccessful effort at armed revolt (the tactic preferred in general by the Chinese Communists). Castro's Cuba had declined to take sides in the Sino-Soviet dispute, torn between Soviet aid and Chinese anti-American militancy. But the Chinese were not content with this and in 1965 tried to use their advisers in Cuba to disseminate their own propaganda in the Cuban armed forces and elsewhere, according to Castro. Moreover, he maintained, they had withheld promised rice deliveries from the impoverished Cuban economy. Moreover, the Cuban fiasco was not the last Chinese setback in 1966. In August the North Korean regime announced what amounted to a neutralist position—rejection of the patronage of any great power. With the Communists of Vietnam increasingly dependent on the Soviet Union and the Indonesian Communists in eclipse, the Korean departure signalled the dissolution of the Asian Communist grouping that had followed the Chinese leadership in 1964-1965.

By disavowing the policy of head-on collision with the Chinese, the Brezhnev leadership had relaxed the attitude of many foreign Communists toward the Soviet Union, while making the Chinese appear increasingly unreasonable. Where Khrushchev had unwittingly pushed some of the foreign parties into a pro-Chinese, or at least anti-Soviet, position, Brezhnev enabled his party to appear relatively tolerant, no longer dangerous to the sovereignty of the smaller parties. This was a net gain for the Soviets, but it represented neither victory over the stubborn Chinese nor any fundamental advance toward a realization of the Marxian myth of international proletarian unity. The Soviets and Chinese alike professed to be patient regarding the ultimate triumph of their own, "correct" ideas, but this aimless outlook merely served to emphasize the exhaustion of their ability to seek either a genuine reconciliation or a so-called victory.

The
Albanian Affair

DOCUMENT 23

*Declaration of the Central Committee of
the Albanian Party of Labor,
October 20, 1961.*

N. KHRUSHCHEV ATTACKED the Albanian Party of Labor publicly at the 22nd Congress of the Communist Party of the Soviet Union.* The anti-Marxist slanders and attacks of N. Khrushchev serve only the enemies of Communism and the Albanian People's Republic—the various imperialists and the Yugoslav revisionists. N. Khrushchev, by revealing to the enemies the differences which have long existed between the leadership of the Communist Party of the Soviet Union and the Albanian Party of Labor, brutally violated the 1960 Moscow Declaration, which stresses that differences arising between fraternal parties should be settled patiently in the spirit of pro-

From William E. Griffith, *Albania and the Sino-Soviet Dispute* (Cambridge, Mass.: M.I.T. Press, 1963), pp. 228-230 (in the series "Studies in International Communism" of the Center for International Studies of the Massachusetts Institute of Technology). Reprinted by permission of the publisher. © 1963 by the Massachusetts Institute of Technology. All rights reserved.

* Reference is to Khrushchev's report as first secretary, which was delivered on October 17. See Leo Gruliow (ed.), *Current Soviet Policies IV* (New York: Columbia University Press, 1962), pp. 42-77.

letarian internationalism and on the basis of the principles of equality and consultations. By attacking the Albanian Party of Labor publicly, N. Khrushchev in fact began an open attack against the unity of the international Communist and workers movement, against the unity of the socialist camp. N. Khrushchev bears full responsibility for this anti-Marxist act and for all the consequences which may follow.

Guided by the interests of the unity of the international Communist movement and the socialist camp, the Albanian Party of Labor has, since the beginning of our differences with the Soviet leadership, tried with great patience to resolve them in the correct Marxist-Leninist way, the way emphasized by the Moscow Declaration. N. Khrushchev, however, chose the anti-Marxist path of aggravating them—the path of attacks and slanders, of pressure and threats, and of the public airing of our differences.

The Albanian Party of Labor received with sympathy the statement of Comrade Chou En-lai, head of the delegation of the Communist Party of China, at the 22nd Congress of the Communist Party of the Soviet Union, which pointed out that unilateral criticism and public airing of differences existing between fraternal parties before our enemies cannot be considered a serious Marxist-Leninist attitude. However, from the rostrum of the 22nd Congress of the Communist Party of the Soviet Union, even after this principled admonition by the representative of the Communist Party of China, the most vicious attacks and slanders against the Albanian Party of Labor and the Albanian People's Republic are being meted out by certain members of the Soviet leadership and by certain leaders of the Communist and workers parties of other countries. Thus they too are assuming a heavy historical responsibility as the disrupters of the unity of the international Communist and workers movement. . . .

The unity of the socialist camp and the international Communist and workers movement is being seriously endangered by the anti-Marxist activities of N. Khrushchev and his followers. In this situation, the Albanian Party of Labor, with a clear conscience, has assumed and will assume all responsibility before the international Communist and workers movement and before the Albanian people for any action which it may take to defend the lofty interests of the people, the fatherland, and their socialist victories and to safeguard the purity of Marxism-Leninism and the unity of the ranks of the Communist movement and the socialist camp.

The struggle which is being imposed upon our party and people will be long and difficult. But difficulties have never frightened our party and people. Our party and people have been tempered in the struggle against the slanders, attacks, and numerous and repeated plots of the various imperialist and Yugoslav revisionists. They will likewise neither bend nor fall on their knees before the slanderous attacks, blackmail, and pressures of N. Khrushchev and his followers. Our party and our people, with their steel-like unity, will as always march resolutely forward and will triumph on their correct road, the road of the triumph of Marxism-Leninism and the cause of socialism and Communism. We will win because we are not alone. With us, and with the great cause of Marxism-Leninism, are the Communists and the peoples of the Soviet Union, who are linked to us by an indestructible love and friendship which we will always preserve intact in our hearts regardless of storm or stress; with us are the Communists and the people of China, all the Communists of the world, and the peoples of the other socialist countries. The victorious banner of the party, the invincible banner of Marxism-Leninism, will always wave proudly in the new socialist Albania.

Signed: The Central Committee
of the Albanian Party of Labor.

DOCUMENT 24

Khrushchev's Concluding Speech to the Soviet Party Congress, October 27, 1961.

. . . COMRADES! THE CENTRAL COMMITTEE's report and also speeches by delegates to the Congress have referred to the erroneous position of the leaders of the Albanian Party of Labor, who have taken the path of combating the line of our party's 20th Congress and undermining the foundations of friendship with the Soviet Union and other socialist countries.

The representatives of the fraternal parties have declared in their speeches that they share our alarm over the state of affairs in the Albanian Party of Labor and roundly condemn the dangerous actions of its leaders, which are prejudicing the fundamental interests of the Albanian people and the solidarity of the entire socialist commonwealth. The speeches by delegates and by representatives of the fraternal parties are convincing evidence that our party's Central Committee was absolutely correct in reporting to the Congress, openly and as a matter of principle, on the abnormal state of Soviet-Albanian relations.

From *The Current Digest of the Soviet Press* (published weekly at Columbia University), Vol. GIII, no. 46, pp. 25-27. © 1961 by The Joint Committee on Slavic Studies and reprinted by permission of *The Current Digest of the Soviet Press*. Originally in *Pravda*, October 29, pp. 1-3.

We were obliged to do this because our repeated attempts to normalize relations with the Albanian Party of Labor have unfortunately borne no fruit. I should like to emphasize that the Central Committee of our party has shown a maximum of patience and has done everything in its power to restore good relations between our parties. . . .

Our great party has more than once been subjected to bitter and filthy attacks from open and covert enemies of communism. But it must be said outright that we do not recall an instance in which anyone shifted with such dizzying speed from protestations and vows of eternal friendship to unbridled anti-Soviet slander as the Albanian leaders have done.

Presumably they expect in this way to lay the groundwork for earning handouts from the imperialists. The imperialists are always willing to pay thirty pieces of silver to those who cause a split in the ranks of the Communists. But pieces of silver have never brought anyone anything but dishonor and shame. (*Applause.*) . . .

Comrade Chou En-lai, head of the delegation of the Communist Party of China, voiced concern in his speech over our having openly raised the issue of Albanian-Soviet relations at the Congress. As far as we can see, his statement primarily reflects alarm lest the present state of our relations with the Albanian Party of Labor affect the solidarity of the socialist camp.

We share the anxiety of our Chinese friends and appreciate their concern for the strengthening of unity. If the Chinese comrades wish to apply their efforts to normalizing the Albanian Party of Labor's relations with the fraternal parties, it is doubtful whether there is anyone better able to facilitate accomplishment of this purpose than the Communist Party of China. This would really redound to the benefit of the Albanian Party of Labor and accord with the interests of the entire commonwealth of socialist countries. (*Prolonged applause.*) . . .

Why did the Albanian leaders launch a campaign against the decisions of our party's 20th Congress? What treason do they see in them?

Above all, the resolute condemnation of the Stalin cult and its harmful consequences is not to the liking of the Albanian leaders. They are displeased that we should have resolutely denounced the arbitrary rule, the abuse of power from which many innocent people suffered, among them eminent representatives of the old guard who had been with Lenin in building the world's first proletarian state. The Albanian leaders cannot refer without vexation and rancor to the fact that we have put an end for good to the situation where one man at his own pleasure arbitrarily decided all-important questions relating to the life of our party and country. (*Prolonged applause.*) . . .

One would have supposed that the Leninist line of the 20th Party Congress, which was supported by the fraternal parties, would have met with support from the leadership of the Albanian Party of Labor too, since the cult of the individual is incompatible with Marxism-Leninism. Actually, the Albanian leaders heaped encomiums on the Stalin cult and launched a violent campaign against the decisions of the 20th Party Congress, in an effort to make the socialist countries swerve from this sound course. This, naturally, was no accident. All that was reprehensible in our country in the period of the cult of the individual is manifested in its worst form in the Albanian Party of Labor. It is now an open secret that the Albanian leaders remain in power by resorting to force and arbitrary rule. . . .

The Central Committee of the CPSU has received more than one letter from Albanian Communists appealing to us to restrain the Albanian leaders from dealing savagely with the finest sons and daughters of the Albanian Party of Labor. The delegates to the Congress can form their own idea of the Albanian leaders' moral complexion by having a look at some of these letters.

The Albanian leaders reproach us with meddling in the internal affairs of the Albanian Party of Labor. I should like to tell you what form this so-called meddling took.

A few years ago the Central Committee of the CPSU interceded with the Albanian leaders over the fate of Liri Gega, a former member of the Politburo of the Central Committee of the Albanian Party of Labor, who had been sentenced to death along with her husband. This woman had for a number of years been a member of leading bodies of the Albanian Party of Labor and had taken part in the Albanian people's struggle for liberation. In approaching the Albanian leaders at the time, we were guided by considerations of humanity, by anxiety to prevent the shooting of a woman, and a pregnant woman at that. We felt and still feel that as a fraternal party we had a right to state our opinion in the matter. After all, even in the blackest days of rampant reaction, the tsarist satraps, who tortured revolutionaries, scrupled to execute pregnant women. And here, in a socialist country, they had sentenced to death and they executed a woman who was about to become a mother; they had shown altogether unwarranted cruelty. (*Stir in the hall. Shouts of "Shame! Shame!"*)

People of integrity today incur punishment in Albania just for daring to come out for Soviet-Albanian friendship, which the Albanian leaders are fond of talking about in such highsounding and florid terms. . . .

This is the atmosphere that prevails in the Albanian Party of Labor, and this is why the Albanian leaders oppose the Leninist line of the 20th Party Congress. After all, to put an end to the cult of the individual would in effect mean that Shehu, Hoxha, and others would have to give up their key positions in the Party and government. And this they do not want to do. But we are certain the time will come when the Albanian Communists and the Albanian people will have their say, and then the Albanian leaders will have to answer for the harm they have done their country, their people, and the cause of socialist construction in Albania. (*Stormy, prolonged applause.*) . . .

Attempted
Economic Integration

DOCUMENT 25

Comecon Declaration on "Basic Principles of the International Socialist Division of Labor," June 7, 1962.

. . . THE WORLD SOCIALIST system is a social, economic and political community of free, sovereign nations following the path of socialism and communism, united by common interests and goals and by indestructible ties of international socialist solidarity.

The close union of the socialist countries within a single system is necessitated by the objective laws of economic and political development.

The community of the socialist countries is based on the existence in all of them of an identical economic foundation—public ownership of the means of production, an identical political system—the power of the people headed by the working class, and an identical ideology—Marxism-Leninism. . . .

There exist and are being perfected a variety of forms of economic co-operation and mutual assistance between the socialist countries: co-ordination of national economic plans, production specialization and co-operation, international socialist trade, credits, technical assistance, scientific and tech-

From *New Times*, no. 27, 1962.

nical co-operation, co-operation in economic projects, development of natural resources, etc. The organizational basis of economic co-operation between the socialist countries is also continuously being perfected; the collective body in charge of this co-operation—the Council of Mutual Economic Assistance—has been strengthened. . . .

The experience of the world socialist economic system has shown that at the present stage co-ordination of national economic plans is the principal means for extending international socialist division of labour and pooling the productive efforts of the socialist countries.

Plan co-ordination is a voluntary effort of the socialist countries in joint planning, the aim being maximum utilization of the political and economic advantages of the socialist system to accelerate the building of socialism and communism. It helps to implement the policy of the Communist and Workers' Parties, based on the scientific principles of Marxism-Leninism and a profound analysis of economic potentialities and needs. . . .

Further improvement of international socialist division of labour on the basis of plan co-ordination calls for accelerated development of such advanced forms as specialization and co-operation of production within the socialist camp. Interstate specialization implies concentrating production of similar products in one or several socialist countries so as to meet the needs of all interested countries, thus improving industrial techniques and management, and establishing stable economic ties and co-operation. International specialization should serve to expand production, reduce costs, raise productivity and improve quality and technical standards. . . .

International socialist division of labor raises the efficiency of social production and thus facilitates successful accomplishment of the economic and political tasks set by the Communist and Workers' Parties at each stage of historical development.

The efficiency of social production in the world socialist system manifests itself in a high and steady rate of expansion, enabling progressively fuller satisfaction of the rising requirements of the population of all the socialist countries, and evening out of their economic levels. . . .

When they set out to build socialist society, the countries of the world socialist system differed in level of development of their productive forces. The very nature of socialism dictates evening out of these levels. The world's highest living standards for all the socialist nations and their more or less simultaneous transition to communism are possible only through creation of the production facilities necessary for this. The material conditions for the building of communism are created by the labor effort of the people of the given country, their ever-increasing contribution to the common cause of strengthening the socialist system.

Elimination of differences in economic development levels makes for increased utilization of the advantages of international socialist division of labor and at the same time accelerates the rate of economic development of the entire socialist system. It helps properly to balance extended reproduction within the framework of the world socialist system. . . .

International socialist division of labor is the basis for trade between the socialist countries, which is carried out on the principle of equivalent exchange.

The planned extension of division of labor between the socialist countries can be assisted by the proper organization of commodity deliveries and payments on the world socialist market. As division of labor progresses, it will be necessary to perfect the forms of commodity and monetary relations between the socialist countries. . . .

The basic principles of international socialist division of labor are an expression of the general trends in the development of the world system of socialism. They stem from the nature of the relations between the socialist states, from the levels they have attained in the development of thir productive forces and economic co-operation, and take into account the specific economic and political tasks facing the individual countries and the world socialist system as a whole.

As economic co-operation between the socialist countries grows in strength and scope and more experience is gained in international specialization and co-operation of production, the principles of international socialist division of labor formulated here will be perfected, elaborated and enlarged.

Document 26

"Statement on the Stand of the Rumanian Workers' Party concerning the Problems of the World Communist and Working Class Movement," April 22, 1964 (Part I).

. . . The economic and technical-scientific progress of the socialist countries relies on the relations of cooperation and mutual assistance established

From Agerpres (Rumanian News Agency): *Documents, Articles and Information on Rumania—Supplement*, April, 1964. Because the above material relates directly to the preceding document, it is inserted here as "Part I" of the "Statement." "Part II" appears below, pp. 165-66, as Document 49.

between them. These fruitful relations have seen a steady development; they have proved their efficiency, making a particularly important contribution to the successes scored by the socialist countries.

With a view to the complete utilization of the advantages of these relations, the Council of Mutual Economic Assistance was set up. According to its Rules, its aim is to contribute, through the uniting coordination of efforts, to the development of the national economy, to speeding up economic and technical progress, to raising the level of industrialization of the less developed countries, to the steady increase in labor productivity, and to the ceaseless improvement in the welfare of the peoples in the member countries.

Cooperation within CMEA is achieved on the basis of the principles of fully equal rights, of observance of national sovereignty and interests, of mutual advantage and comradely assistance. . . .

During the development of the relations of cooperation between the socialist countries which are members of CMEA, forms and measures have been suggested, such as a joint plan and a single planning body for all member countries, interstate technical-productive branch unions, enterprises jointly owned by several countries, interstate economic complexes, etc.

Our Party has very clearly expressed its point of view, declaring that, since the essence of the suggested measures lies in shifting some functions of economic management from the competence of the respective state to the attribution of superstate bodies or organisms, these measures are not in keeping with the principles which underlie the relations between the socialist countries.

The idea of a single planning body for all CMEA countries has the most serious economic and political implications. The planned management of the national economy is one of the fundamental, essential, and inalienable attributes of the sovereignty of the socialist state—the state plan being the chief means through which the socialist state achieves its political and socio-economic objectives, establishes the directions and rates of development of the national economy, its fundamental proportions, the accumulations, the measures for raising the people's living standard, and cultural level. The sovereignty of the socialist state requires that it effectively and fully avails itself of the means for the practical implementation of these attributions, holding in its hands all the levers of managing economic and social life. Transmitting such levers to the competence of superstate or extrastate bodies would turn sovereignty into a notion without any contents. . . .

Undoubtedly if some socialist countries deem it fit to adopt in the direct relations between them forms of cooperation different from those unanimously agreed upon within CMEA, that is a question which exclusively concerns those countries, and can be decided by them alone in a sovereign way.

In the present conditions, when there are 14 socialist countries in the world [counting Cuba—ED.], and only some of them are CMEA members, so that the latter's structure only partially reflects the configuration of the world socialist system, an aim that would contribute to the development of economic cooperation between all socialist countries would be that, together with those not belonging to CMEA at present, the best ways be found for the participation in CMEA of all socialist countries, that the broadest and most flexible forms and methods of cooperation be secured which should attract more and more states and facilitate their inclusion, in step with the progress of the world revolutionary process. In this way, CMEA would meet to the highest degree the interests of enhancing the economic might of the socialist community, fully using the advantages of the transformation of socialism into a world system and securing a firm material base to the unity of the socialist countries. Moreover, we consider that forms and methods of participation in CMEA activity have to be found even for those countries that proceed along the path of non-capitalist development in the domains that would be of interest to them.

As to the Rumanian Workers' Party, it steadfastly stands for the strengthening and extension of cooperation with all the socialist countries, for the implementation of the socialist international division of labor within the whole socialist economic system as an objective necessity of developing this system.

At the same time, the socialist international division of labor cannot mean isolation of the socialist countries from the general framework of world economic relations. Standing consistently for normal, mutually advantageous economic relations, without political strings and without restrictions or discriminations, the Rumanian People's Republic, like the other socialist states, develops its economic links with all states irrespective of their social system. . . .

The
Sino-Soviet Correspondence

DOCUMENT 27

*Letter from the Central Committee of the
Communist Party of the Soviet Union to the
Central Committee of the Communist
Party of China, March 30, 1963.*

DEAR COMRADES,

The Central Committee of the Communist Party of the Soviet Union notes with satisfaction that our proposals on measures aimed at strengthening unity and solidarity in the ranks of the communist movement have met with a favorable response on the part of the Central Committee of the Communist Party of China. We welcome your agreement to the holding of a meeting between representatives of the CPSU and CPC. This meeting is called upon to play an important part in creating a favorable atmosphere in relations between the fraternal Parties and in smoothing out the differences which have arisen in recent times in the world communist movement. We would like to hope that as a result of this meeting it will be possible to carry out a number of constructive measures to surmount existing difficulties.

In its letter the CPC Central Committee invites Comrade N.S. Khrushchev to visit Peking en route to Cambodia. The CPSU Central Committee and Comrade N.S. Khrushchev express gratitude for this invitation. Comrade N.S. Khrushchev would with great pleasure visit the People's Republic of China, and meet the leadership of the Communist Party of China to exchange views on urgent questions of the international situation and of the communist movement with the object of achieving a common understanding of our tasks and strengthening solidarity between our Parties. However, it is not in fact planned that Comrade N.S. Khrushchev will make a tour of Cambodia as you mention in your letter. As we all know, in con-

From *Peking Review*, no. 25, 1963. A previous Soviet letter of February 21 and a Chinese reply of March 9, 1963, appear in *Peking Review*, no. 12, 1963.

formity with a decision passed by our leading bodies on February 12, 1963, Comrade L.I. Brezhnev, President of the Presidium of the U.S.S.R. Supreme Soviet, will travel to Cambodia, as the Cambodian Government has already been notified and has been announced in the press. Comrade N.S. Khrushchev, who has already visited the People's Republic of China three times, does not lose hope of availing himself of your kind invitation in the future to visit China and meet the Chinese comrades.

We remember that during his stay in Moscow in 1957 Comrade Mao Tse-tung said that he had only been in the U.S.S.R. twice and had only visited Moscow and Leningrad. He expressed the desire to visit the Soviet Union again to become better acquainted with our country. He said then that he would like to travel from the Far Eastern borders of our country to the western borders, and from the northern to the southern borders. We welcomed this desire of Comrade Mao Tse-tung.

The CPSU Central Committee sent a letter to Comrade Mao Tse-tung on May 12, 1960, inviting him to come and spend a holiday in the U.S.S.R. and familiarize himself with the life of the Soviet people. Unfortunately, Comrade Mao Tse-tung could not at that time avail himself of our invitation. The CPSU Central Committee would welcome a visit by Comrade Mao Tse-tung. The best time for such a visit would be the approaching spring or summer, which are the good seasons of the year in our country. We are also ready at any other time to give a worthy reception to Comrade Mao Tse-tung as a representative of a fraternal Party and of the fraternal Chinese people. In this tour of our country, Comrade Mao Tse-tung would not, of course, be alone. Comrades from the leadership of our Party would go with him, and it would be a fine opportunity for an exchange of opinion on different questions. Comrade Mao Tse-tung would be able to see how the Soviet people are working, and what successes they have scored in the construction of communism and in the implementation of the Program of our Party.

If a visit by Comrade Mao Tse-tung to Moscow cannot take place at present, we are ready to accept your ideas about a top-level meeting between representatives of the CPSU and CPC in Moscow. We believe that a meeting of this kind could take place around May 15, 1963, if this date is acceptable to you. . . .

It goes without saying that when our two Parties are discussing questions concerning all fraternal Parties, the discussion can only be of a preliminary nature. The 1957 and 1960 Meetings have shown that the elaboration of the policy of the international communist movement can be successful only if all fraternal Parties collectively take part in it and if due consideration is given to the extensive experience of all its component detachments.

We have attentively studied your views concerning the range of questions which could be discussed at the meeting of representatives of the Communist Party of the Soviet Union and the Communist Party of China. These are important questions, and we are ready to discuss them.

In our turn, we would like to dwell in this letter on some questions of principle, which, in our opinion, are the center of attention of the fraternal Parties and their struggle for our common cause. We do not mean, of course, an exhaustive statement of our views on these questions. We only wish to note that which is of paramount importance, by which we are guided in our policy in the international arena and in our relations with fraternal Parties.

We hope that this statement of our views will help to define the range of questions requiring an exchange of opinions at a bilateral meeting and will contribute to overcoming the existing differences. We are doing this so as to stress once again our determination to uphold firmly and consistently the ideological standpoint of the entire world communist movement, its general line as expressed in the Declaration and the Statement.

During the time that has passed since the adoption of the Statement, experience has not only not invalidated any of its main conclusions, but has, on the contrary, fully confirmed the correctness of the course taken by the world communist movement, as worked out jointly through generalization of present-day experience and the creative development of Marxism-Leninism.

The Communist Party of the Soviet Union proceeds from the basis that our epoch, whose main content is the transition from capitalism to socialism, initiated by the Great October Socialist Revolution, is an epoch of struggle between two opposed social systems, an epoch of socialist revolutions and national-liberation revolutions, an epoch of the collapse of imperialism, of the abolition of the colonial system, an epoch of transition to socialism by ever more nations, of the triumph of socialism and communism on a world scale. . . .

If Communists were to start tying up the victory of the socialist revolution with world war, this would not evoke any sympathy for socialism, but would drive the masses away from it. With modern means of warfare having such terrible destructive consequences, an appeal like this would only play into the hands of our enemies.

The working class and its vanguard, the Marxist-Leninist parties, endeavor to carry out socialist revolutions in a peaceful way without civil war. The realization of such a possibility is in keeping with the interests of the working class and all the people, and with the national interests of the country. At the same time the choice of the means of developing the revolution depends not only on the working class. If the exploiting classes resort to violence against the people, the working class will be forced to use non-peaceful means of seizing power. Everything depends on the particular conditions and on the distribution of class forces within the country and in the world arena. . . .

The CPSU regards fraternal alliance with the peoples who have shaken off the colonial yoke and with the peoples of semi-colonial states as one of the cornerstones of its international policy. Our Party considers it its international duty to help the peoples who have taken the road of winning and consolidating national independence, all the peoples fighting for the complete abolition of the colonial system. The Soviet Union has always supported the sacred wars of the peoples for freedom, and given every kind of moral, economic, military and political support to the national-liberation movement. . . .

In your letter, dear comrades, you justly note that the guarantee of all our achievements is the strengthening of the unity of the communist movement and the solidarity of the socialist countries. In recent time the CPSU has at its congresses and at international communist meetings time and again expressed its conception of the principles concerning the relations between Marxist-Leninist parties. We emphasized, for the whole world to see, that in the communist movement, just as in the socialist community, all Communist and Workers' Parties, of all socialist countries have always been completely equal. In the communist movement there are no "higher ranking" and "subordinate" Parties. And it could not be so. The domination of any Party, or the manifestation of any hegemony whatsoever, does not benefit the international communist and workers' movement; on the contrary, it can only do it harm. All Communist Parties are independent and equal. All bear responsibility for the destiny of the communist movement, for its victories and setbacks, all must build their relations on the basis of proletarian internationalism and mutual assistance.

We also proceed from the basis that proletarian internationalism places equal demands on all Parties, big and small, but makes no exceptions for any one. All fraternal Parties must show equal concern that their activities be based on Marxist-Leninist principles, in accordance with the interests of strengthening the unity of the socialist countries and of the entire world communist and workers' movement. . . .

Being firmly convinced that the present policy of the international communist movement, which found its expression in the Declaration and Statement of the fraternal Parties, is the only correct one, we believe that at the forthcoming meeting between the representativs of the CPSU and CPC it would be expedient to discuss the following most urgent problems:

a) Questions concerning the struggle for the further strengthening of the might of the world socialist system and its transformation into the decisive factor in the development of human society, which is the main distinguishing feature of our era. . . .

b) Questions concerning the struggle for peace and peaceful coexistence. . . .

c) Questions concerning the struggle against imperialism headed by the U.S. . . .

d) Questions concerning the national-liberation movement. The support and utmost development of the national-liberation movement of the peoples. . . .

e) Questions concerning the consolidation of the unity and cohesion of the socialist commonwealth and of the ranks of the communist movement. . . .

During the talks it will be possible to discuss all the questions mentioned in your letter, questions of common interest stemming from the tasks in the struggle to implement the decisions of the Moscow Meetings. An important role could be played by the discussion of the questions connected with the consolidation of unity between the U.S.S.R. and the People's Republic of China.

In your letter you raise the Albanian and Yugoslav questions. We have already written to you that these questions, though of a basic nature, cannot and should not eclipse the main problems of our times which call for discussion at our meeting.

Our Party, having condemned the splitting activities of the Albanian leaders, has at the same time taken a number of steps towards normalizing the relations between the Albanian Party of Labor and the CPSU and other fraternal Parties. In spite of the fact that the leaders of the Albanian Party of Labor have recently been coming out with slanderous attacks on our Party and the Soviet people, we, being guided by supreme interests, do not relinquish the hope that the relations between the CPSU and the Albanian Party of Labor may be improved. At the end of February this year the CPSU Central Committee once again took the initiative and suggested to the Central Committee of the Albanian Party of Labor that a bilateral meeting be held between representatives of our two Parties. However, this comradely step on our part did not meet with due response on the part of the Albanian leadership. The leaders of the Albanian Party of Labor did not even deem it necessary to acknowledge our letter containing the CPSU Central Committee's proposal about the bilateral meetings. Having obviously later come to their senses, the Albanian leaders sent us a letter in which, after some reservations and stipulations, they speak of such a meeting. If real desire is in fact shown, we are ready to have a meeting.

As far as Yugoslavia is concerned, we maintain, proceeding from an analysis and assessment of the objective economic and political conditions in that country, that it is a socialist country, and in our relations with it we strive to establish closer relations between the Federative People's Republic of Yugoslavia and the socialist commonwealth, in accordance with the policy pursued by the fraternal Parties for the cementing together of all the anti-imperialist forces of the world. We also take into consideration the definite positive tendencies shown of late in Yugoslavia's economic and socio-political life. Meanwhile the CPSU is aware of the serious differences that exist with the League of Communists of Yugoslavia on several ideological questions and considers it necessary to tell the Yugoslav comrades so frankly, criticizing those views of theirs which it finds wrong. . . .

Our Party does not succumb to the heat of the polemic struggle but, aware of our common responsibility to the world communist movement, wishes to stop the dangerous process of sliding into a new series of discussions. It is obvious to everyone that we could have found much to say in defence of the Leninist policy of the CPSU, in defence of the common line of the international communist movement, in reply to groundless attacks made in articles recently carried by the Chinese press. And if we are not doing it now it is only because we do not want to gladden the foes of the communist movement. We hope that the harm caused by the sharpening polemics will be realized, and the interests of the unity of the socialist system and the international communist movement will be placed above all else. Therefore we suggest a meeting to you, not in order to aggravate the dispute but in order to reach a mutual understanding on major problems that have arisen in the international communist movement.

We know that such a meeting is being looked forward to by our friends in all the countries of the world, and that they pin great hopes on it. It depends on us, on our will and reason, whether results gladdening to our friends and upsetting to the enemies of communism will be achieved at the meeting. This will be our common contribution to the cause of the struggle for the liberation of all oppressed people, for the victory of peace and socialism on earth, for the triumph of the great revolutionary doctrine of Marxism-Leninism.

With communist greetings,

The Central Committee
of the Communist Party of the Soviet Union

DOCUMENT 28

*Letter from the Central Committee of the
Communist Party of China to the Central
Committee of the Communist Party of
the Soviet Union, June 14, 1963.*

DEAR COMRADES! The Central Committee of the Communist Party of
China has studied the letter of the Central Committee of the Communist
Party of the Soviet Union of March 30, 1963. . . .

In its letter of March 30, the Central Committee of the CPSU systemat-
ically presents its views on questions that need to be discussed in the talks
between the Chinese and Soviet Parties, and in particular raises the question of the general line of the international Communist movement. In this
letter we too would like to express our views, which constitute our proposal
on the general line of the international Communist movement and on some
related questions of principle.

We hope that this exposition of views will be conducive to mutual understanding by our two parties and to a detailed, point-by-point discussion in
the talks.

We also hope that this will be conducive to the understanding of our
views by the fraternal parties and to a full exchange of ideas at an international meeting of fraternal parties.

1. It is true that for several years there have been differences within the
international Communist movement in the understanding of, and the attitude toward, the Declaration of 1957 and the Statement of 1960. The
central issue here is whether or not to accept the revolutionary principles
of the Declaration and the Statement. In the last analysis, it is a question
of whether or not to accept the universal truth of Marxism-Leninism,
whether or not to recognize the universal significance of the road of the
October Revolution, whether or not to accept the fact that the people still
living under the imperialist and capitalist system, who comprise two-thirds
of the world's population, need to make revolution, and whether or not to
accept the fact that the people already on the socialist road, who comprise
one-third of the world's population, need to carry their revolution forward
to the end. . . .

From *Peking Review*, no. 25, 1963. This letter was published in the Soviet Union only on July 14, 1963, along with an open letter from the Central Committee of the CPSU to members of the party. See *The Current Digest of the
Soviet Press,* vol. XV, no. 28.

3. If the general line of the international Communist movement is one-sidely reduced to "peaceful coexistence," "peaceful competition," and "peaceful transition," this is to violate the revolutionary principles of the 1957 Declaration and the 1960 Statement, to discard the historical mission of proletarian world revolution and to depart from the revolutionary teachings of Marxism-Leninism. . . .

8. The various types of contradictions in the contemporary world are concentrated in the vast areas of Asia, Africa, and Latin America; these are the most vulnerable areas under imperialist rule and the storm centers of world revolution dealing direct blows at imperialism.

The national democratic revolutionary movement in these areas and the international socialist revolutionary movement are the two great historical currents of our time.

The national democratic revolution in these areas is an important component of the contemporary proletarian world revolution.

The anti-imperialist revolutionary struggles of the people in Asia, Africa, and Latin America are pounding and undermining the foundations of the rule of imperialism and colonialism, old and new, and are now a mighty force in defense of world peace.

In a sense, therefore, the whole cause of the international proletarian revolution hinges on the outcome of the revolutionary struggles of the people of these areas, who constitute the overwhelming majority of the world's population. . . .

15. The complete banning and destruction of nuclear weapons is an important task in the struggle to defend world peace. We must do our utmost to this end.

Nuclear weapons are unprecedentedly destructive, which is why for more than a decade now the U.S. imperialists have been pursuing their policy of nuclear blackmail in order to realize their ambition of enslaving the people of all countries and dominating the world. . . .

In the view of Marxist-Leninists, the people are the makers of history. In the present, as in the past, man is the decisive factor. Marxist-Leninists attach importance to the role of technological change, but it is wrong to belittle the role of man and exaggerate the role of technology.

The emergence of nuclear weapons can neither arrest the progress of human history nor save the imperialist system from its doom, any more than the emergence of new techniques could save the old systems from their doom in the past.

The emergence of nuclear weapons does not and cannot resolve the fundamental contradictions in the contemporary world, does not and cannot alter the law of class struggle, and does not and cannot change the nature of imperialism and reaction. . . .

18. Both Marx and Lenin maintained that the entire period before the advent of the higher stage of communist society is the period of transition from capitalism to communism, the period of the dictatorship of the proletariat. In this transition period, the dictatorship of the proletariat—that is to say, the proletarian state—goes through the dialectical process of establishment, consolidation, strengthening, and withering away. . . .

Certain persons may say that their society is already one without classes. We answer: No, there are classes and class struggles in all socialist countries without exception.

Since remnants of the old exploiting classes who are trying to stage a comeback still exist there, since new capitalist elements are constantly being generated there, and since there are still parasites, speculators, idlers, hooligans, embezzlers of state funds, etc., how can it be said that classes or class struggles no longer exist? How can it be said that the dictatorship of the proletariat is no longer necessary? . . .

In calling a socialist state the "state of the entire people," [a label that Khrushchev had applied to the U.S.S.R.—ED.] is one trying to replace the Marxist-Leninist theory of the state by the bourgeois theory of the state? Is one trying to replace the state of the dictatorship of the proletariat by a state of a different character?

If that is the case, it is nothing but a great historical retrogression. The degeneration of the social system in Yugoslavia is a grave lesson.

20. Over the past few years, certain persons have violated Lenin's integral teachings about the interrelationship of leaders, party, class, and masses, and raised the issue of "combating the cult of the individual"; this is erroneous and harmful. . . .

The Communist Party of China has always disapproved of exaggerating the role of the individual, has advocated and persistently practiced democratic centralism within the Party, and advocated the linking of the leadership with the masses, maintaining that correct leadership must know how to concentrate the views of the masses.

While loudly combating the so-called cult of the individual, certain persons are in reality doing their best to defame the proletarian party and the dictatorship of the proletariat. At the same time, they are enormously exaggerating the role of certain individuals, shifting all errors onto others and claiming all credit for themselves.

What is more serious is that, under the pretext of "combating the cult of the individual," certain persons are crudely interfering in the internal affairs of other fraternal parties and fraternal countries and forcing other fraternal parties to change their leadership in order to impose their own wrong line on these parties. What is all this if not great-power chauvinism, sectarianism and splittism? What is all this if not subversion?

It is high time to propagate seriously and comprehensively Lenin's integral teachings on the interrelationship of leaders, party, class and masses.

21. Relations between socialist countries are international relations of a new type. Relations between socialist countries, whether large or small, and whether more developed or less developed economically, must be based on the principles of complete equality, respect for territorial integrity, sovereignty, and independence, and noninterference in each other's internal affairs, and must also be based on the principles of mutual support and mutual assistance in accordance with proletarian internationalism. . . .

It would be great-power chauvinism to deny these basic principles and, in the name of "international division of labor" or "specialization," to impose one's own will on others, infringe on the independence and sovereignty of fraternal countries or harm the interests of their people. . . .

22. The 1957 Declaration and the 1960 Statement lay down the principles guiding relations among fraternal parties. These are the principle of solidarity, the principle of mutual support and mutual assistance, the principle of independence and equality and the principle of reaching unanimity through consultation—all on the basis of Marxism-Leninism and proletarian internationalism. . . .

If the principle of reaching unanimity through consultation is accepted in relations among fraternal parties, then one should not emphasize "who is in the majority" or "who is in the minority" and bank on a so-called majority in order to force through one's own erroneous line and carry out sectarian and splitting policies.

If it is agreed that differences between fraternal parties should be settled through inter-Party consultation, then other fraternal parties should not be attacked publicly and by name at one's own Congress or at other Party Congresses, in speeches by Party leaders, resolutions, statements, etc.; and still less should the ideological differences among fraternal parties be extended into the sphere of state relations. . . .

23. In order to carry out the common program of the international Communist movement unanimously agreed upon by the fraternal parties, an uncompromising struggle must be waged against all forms of opportunism, which is a deviation from Marxism-Leninism. . . .

The Declaration and the Statement point out that revisionism, or, in other words, right opportunism, is the main danger in the international Communist movement. Yugoslav revisionism typifies modern revisionism. . . .

It is completely groundless and out of keeping with the facts to assert that Yugoslavia is showing "certain positive trends," that it is a "socialist country," and that the Tito clique is an "anti-imperialist force."

Certain persons are now attempting to introduce the Yugoslav revisionist clique into the socialist community and the international Communist ranks. This is openly to tear up the agreement unanimously reached at the 1960 meeting of the fraternal parties and is absolutely impermissible. . . .

In your letter of March 30, you invited Comrade Mao Tse-tung to visit the Soviet Union. As early as Feb. 23, Comrade Mao Tse-tung in his conversation with the Soviet Ambassador to China clearly stated the reason why he was not prepared to visit the Soviet Union at the present time. You were well aware of this.

When a responsible comrade of the Central Committee of the Communist Party of China received the Soviet Ambassador to China on May 9, he informed you that we would send a delegation to Moscow in the middle of June. Later, in compliance with the request of the Central Committee of the CPSU, we agreed to postpone the talks between our two parties to July 5.

We sincerely hope that the talks between the Chinese and Soviet Parties will yield positive results and contribute to the preparations for convening the meeting of all Communist and Workers' Parties. . . .

Workers of all countries, unite! Workers and oppressed peoples and nations of the world, unite! Oppose our common enemy!

With Communist greetings!

Central Committee
of the Communist Party of China

Document 29

Letter from the Central Committee of the Communist Party of the Soviet Union to the Central Committee of the Communist Party of China, November 29, 1963.

Dear Comrades,

The communist press has recently published documents in which the Marxist-Leninist parties have publicly expounded their positions on fundamental questions of the international communist movement raised in

From *Peking Review*, no. 19, 1964.

the debate that has unfolded. These documents show that there are serious differences in the communist movement, differences in the understanding and interpretation of the fundamental theses of the Declaration and the Statement of the Moscow meetings. We will not conceal the fact that, like many other fraternal parties, irrespective of the position they are taking, we are seriously concerned over the fact that the differences which have arisen are constantly becoming deeper and the scope of the questions under debate is constantly widening, while the sharp public polemics are assuming forms impermissible in relations among Marxist-Leninists. . . .

Of course parties like the CPSU and the CPC, standing at the head of the world's two biggest states, can go on with their work even if the polemics continue. We agree that for our two parties even in such circumstances, as you said to the Soviet Ambassador Comrade Chervonenko, the skies will not fall, and grass and trees will continue to grow, women to bear children, and fish to swim in the water.

But we cannot fail to see that the differences and sharp polemics are doing great harm to the communist movement. We also have no right to fail to think of those detachments of the communist movement which are forced to carry on the struggle against imperialism in extremely difficult and complex circumstances. Such parties rightly consider that they require friendship with both the CPSU and the CPC. All Marxist-Leninist parties draw strength from the unity and solidarity of the communist movement for the overcoming of difficulties.

The communists of all countries want unity of action. And they are right—without unity of action our struggle against class enemies will be many times harder. . . .

Concretely speaking, we propose that notwithstanding the differences we should place at the center of our mutual relations the development of co-operation for the sake of strengthening friendship between the Soviet Union and China and among all the socialist countries and fraternal Marxist-Leninist parties, and of coordinating actions in the various international organizations for our common aim of defending peace and combating imperialism.

Particularly great possibilities exist for the strengthening of ties between the People's Republic of China and the U.S.S.R. in the economic field and in the fields of scientific-technical cooperation and culture. In this letter, we would like to make a series of practical proposals, the realization of which could serve the cause of strengthening friendship between our countries. . . .

You will probably agree that the situation which has arisen in recent years along different sections of the Soviet-Chinese border cannot be regarded as normal. The Soviet government has already proposed that friendly consultations take place to define accurately the boundary in different sections, considering that this will result in removal of the causes of the present misunderstanding. Recently you, too, spoke in favor of solving this question on the basis of mutual consultation. In this connection, we are transmitting to you a relevant document. (Not published—ED.)

Statements have recently been made in China concerning the aggressive policy of the tsarist government and the unjust treaties imposed upon China. Naturally, we will not defend the Russian tsars who permitted arbitrariness in laying down the state boundaries with neighboring countries. We are convinced that you, too, do not intend to defend the Chinese emperors who by force of arms seized not a few territories belonging to others. But while condemning the reactionary actions of the top-strata exploiters who held power in Russia and in China at that time, we cannot disregard that fact that historically-formed boundaries between states now exist. Any attempt to ignore this can become the source of misunderstandings and conflicts; at the same time, they will not lead to the solution of the problem. It would be simply unreasonable to create territorial problems artificially at the present time, when the working class is in power and when our common aim is communism, under which state borders will gradually lose their former significance. We have all the possibilities for fully eliminating border frictions of any kind, and thus showing the peoples an example of truly friendly relations between two socialist states.

We should also create conditions favorable to the improvement of relations on the Party level and avoid anything that might aggravate the difficulties that have arisen in the communist movement. That the overcoming of the differences in the communist movement is a complex matter, demanding time and serious effort, is something we are fully aware of. But what is important is to go step by step in this direction, to show Leninist concern for the strengthening of the unity of the world communist movement on a principled Marxist basis, to bar any acts whatsoever that might undermine unity, and to repulse factionalists and splitters.

We are of the opinion that even in the present complex situation there is a possibility of preventing the polemics that have spread from getting out of control, and of directing matters toward the strengthening of unity and solidarity between the CPC and the CPSU and among all the fraternal parties. The Central Committee of the CPSU has more than once advocated the cessation of public polemics. We again repeated this proposal on October 25 and November 7, 1963. The Soviet press has ceased to publish materials of a polemical character. In this letter we call once more on the Central Committee of the Chinese Communist Party to do everything necessary for the cessation of public polemics and of other activities that harm the unity of the international communist movement and the unity of the socialist countries. We do not propose a general cessation of the exchange of views on questions of principle concerning world developments, but desire only that it should take place in the forms provided for by the statement of the fraternal parties in 1960—through mutual consultation, negotiations, and exchanges of letters. . . .

The Central Committee of the CPSU calls on the Central Committee of the CPC, on its part, to undertake practical steps for the strengthening of the unity of the fraternal parties on the principles of Marxism-Leninism and proletarian internationalism in the struggle for the great cause of socialism.

> First Secretary of the Central Committee
> of the Communist Party of the Soviet Union
> (signed) N. Khrushchev

DOCUMENT 30

Letter from the Central Committee of the Communist Party of China to the Central Committee of the Communist Party of the Soviet Union, February 20, 1964.

DEAR COMRADES,

We have learnt from a number of quarters that the Central Committee of the CPSU recently sent to fraternal parties a letter [not published— ED.] which is directed against the Communist Party of China. This letter distorts the facts of the current public polemics in the international communist movement, manufactures lies slandering the Chinese Communist Party and instigates a so-called "struggle against the great-power and Trotskyite views and the factional and disruptive activities of the Chinese leaders." This letter has not, however, been sent to the Chinese Communist Party, from which it has been kept a secret. . . .

You have launched the present campaign against the Chinese Communist Party on the new pretext that the CPC has not yet replied to your letter of November 29, 1963. But we would like to ask: why were you free for a long time to act wilfully and refuse to accept the advice of fraternal parties

From *Peking Review*, no. 19, 1964.

against bringing inter-party differences into the open before the enemy and their proposal for a halt to public polemics, whereas the CPC must regard the letter from the leaders of the CPSU as God's will and give an immediate and affirmative reply or else be charged with the major crime of insubordination? Why are you privileged to publish thousands of lengthy articles and other items attacking us, whereas we may not make any reply to set the facts straight and distinguish truth from falsehood? A journey has to be made step by step, and problems have to be solved one by one. Your letter will be answered in due course. Your self-important and domineering attitude in maintaining that you can attack whenever you please and that we must stop as soon as you cry halt has fully exposed your inveterate habit of great-power chauvinism and posing as the "father party." . . .

We would like in all seriousness to repeat our request [the Soviets maintained that the Chinese word used here should be translated as "demand" —ED.] that the Central Committee of the CPSU send us a copy of the letter directed against the CPC, which it has recently addressed to fraternal parties. We shall make our reply after studying this letter.

With fraternal greetings,

The Central Committee
of the Communist Party of China

DOCUMENT 31

*Letter from the Central Committee of the
Communist Party of the Soviet Union to the
Central Committee of the Communist
Party of China, February 22, 1964.*

DEAR COMRADES,

The Central Committee of the CPSU has received your letter of February 20, 1964.

The rude tone and the unworthy and insulting methods in relation to the Communist Party of the Soviet Union to which you resort in this letter give us the moral right not to answer it at all. And if we have nevertheless considered it expedient to reply to you, we are doing so only in order to eliminate the possibility of any speculation or attempt to mislead the uninformed.

From *Peking Review,* no. 19, 1964.

You express a simulated indignation at the fact that the letter of the Central Committee of the CPSU dated February 12 this year, addressed to many fraternal parties, was not sent to the Central Committee of the Communist Party of China, and represent this almost as an attempt to conceal the content of this letter from you and as "sectarian" and "factional activity by the CPSU." . . .

While not answering our letters, you at the same time unfolded a widespread campaign against the CPSU and other Marxist-Leninist parties and sharply intensified the schismatic factional activity in the international communist movement and the democratic organizations. In an article on February 4 this year, the newspaper *Jen-min Jih-pao* openly called for a split in the communist movement and demonstrated the unwillingness of the CPC leadership to reply to the positive proposals contained in the letter of the Central Committee of the CPSU dated November 29, 1963.

In these circumstances the Central Committee of the CPSU, in the interests of the unity of the communist movement and desirous of stating its Marxist-Leninist viewpoints which are being libellously assailed by the Chinese press, considered it necessary to discuss the question at the February plenum of the Central Committee and thereafter to state its views openly. The Central Committee of the CPSU decided to inform the fraternal parties of this.

We had to tell them frankly that our proposals had not evoked any positive response from the leaders of the CPC and that the latter, broadening the schismatic activity, were continuing to intensify the attacks on the common cause of the world communist movement. We declared that we shared the opinion of all the fraternal parties standing genuinely on the positions of the Declaration and the Statement that it was necessary to give rebuff to the schismatics and take collective measures for strengthening the unity of the communist movement on the principled basis of Marxism-Leninism. We asserted once more the desirability of calling a meeting of the communist and workers' parties, concerning which you yourselves made repeated declarations at one time.

Our letter condemned the intention of the leadership of the CPC to create a factional bloc with a special program under its own hegemony.

This is what was discussed in the February 12 letter of the Central Committee of the CPSU. . . .

Your great-power habits also appear in your last short letter when, addressing the Central Committee of the CPSU, you demand that it send to you its letter of February 12. You do not request, but demand. One asks, by what right? Can it really be that you consider that anyone will take your tone seriously, become frightened and rush as fast as his legs can carry him to fulfill your every demand? This is not merely rude but simply ridiculous.

Your letter and its deliberately rude tone compels us to reflect once again: with what purpose was it sent? After all, nobody will believe that such an unseemly message was sent in the interests of the strengthening of friendship with the CPSU, of which you ceaselessly talk to your own people and the international communist movement, thus deceiving them. Anyone who acquaints himself with this letter will see that it is aimed at the aggravation of differences and the exacerbation of the situation in the communist movement. . . .

The Central Committee of the CPSU expresses its firm conviction that the world communist movement will overcome the existing difficulties, unite its ranks even more closely under the banner of Marx-Engels-Lenin, and achieve new successes in the struggle for the great cause of the working class, for the victory of the national liberation movement, for the cause of peace and the security of the peoples, for the victory of communism.

With ardent fraternal greetings,

The Central Committee
of the Communist Party of the Soviet Union

DOCUMENT 32

Letter from the Central Committee of the Communist Party of China to the Central Committee of the Communist Party of the Soviet Union, February 27, 1964.

DEAR COMRADES,

The Central Committee of the Communist Party of China has received your letter of February 22, 1964. The characteristic feature of this letter is the prodigality of the abuse—such as "unseemly," "a clumsy attempt to lay one's own fault at somebody else's door," "rude" and "ridiculous"— with which you try to evade the questions of substance which we raised in our letter of February 20, 1964. This is really a poor performance. . . .

You begin your letter with the assertion that you have the "right not to answer at all" the letter of the Central Committee of the CPC to the Cen-

From *Peking Review*, no. 19, 1964.

tral Committee of the CPSU, whereas we have repeatedly made it clear that we will answer your letter of November 29, 1963 in due course. We have advised you against impatience because we have not yet completed our reply to your numerous attacks. Whereupon you have flown into a rage as if we had committed a monstrous crime. Please think the matter over calmly: can this be described as treating fraternal parties as equals? . . .

. . . acting like "knights for a day," you state in your letter that you will "publish documents" and "state our views openly." Moreover, you declared on September 21, 1963 that you would give us a "most resolute rebuff." Have you not played enough of such tricks? Have you not divulged enough information? Were these to be enumerated, we could cite a wealth of facts beginning from the 20th Congress of the CPSU. You are well aware of this and we do not need to waste our ink. Now you are again making an empty threat, and, to be blunt, this can only frighten people with weak nerves. In our opinion, all your bluster simply reminds one of a paper tiger. It is like a pewter-pointed spear. Please produce all the magic weapons in your treasure box for our enlightenment—the "most resolute rebuff," "open statement of our views," "collective measures" against the CPC, documents and materials, and what not. . . .

If you do not fear the truth and the masses and if, instead of treating them as rabble, you have faith in the political consciousness and discernment of the members of the CPSU and the Soviet people, we propose that our two parties reach an agreement, by which each side will, on an equal basis, publish in its own press the documents, articles, and other material both sides have published or will publish in criticism of each other.

You accuse us of committing a blunder by "demanding" instead of "requesting" that you send us a copy of your letter of February 12. In Chinese usage, these two words do not imply as big a difference as you describe. But since you take it so seriously and even make it an excuse for refusing to give us the letter of February 12, which is directed against the CPC, well then, we are now complying with your wish and request that you send us a copy of the letter which you gave the other fraternal parties on February 12. It is our earnest hope that you will do so.

With fraternal greetings,

The Central Committee
of the Communist Party of China

DOCUMENT 33

Letter from the Central Committee of the Communist Party of China to the Central Committee of the Communist Party of the Soviet Union, February 29, 1964.

DEAR COMRADES,

This letter from the Central Committee of the Communist Party of China is in reply to the letter of the Central Committee of the Communist Party of the Soviet Union dated November 29, 1963. . . .

The government of the People's Republic of China has consistently held that the question of the boundary between China and the Soviet Union, which is a legacy from the past, can be settled through negotiation between the two governments. It has also held that, pending such a settlement, the status quo on the border should be maintained. This is what we have done over the past ten years or more. Had the Soviet government taken the same attitude, both sides could have lived in amity along the border and preserved tranquillity there.

With the stepping up of anti-Chinese activities by the leaders of the CPSU in recent years, the Soviet side has made frequent breaches of the status quo on the border, occupied Chinese territory and provoked border incidents. Still more serious, the Soviet side has flagrantly carried out large-scale subversive activities in Chinese frontier areas, trying to sow discord among China's nationalities by means of the press and wireless, inciting China's minority nationalities to break away from their motherland, and inveigling and coercing tens of thousands of Chinese citizens into going to the Soviet Union. Not only do all these acts violate the principles guiding relations between socialist countries, they are absolutely impermissible even in the relations between countries in general.

We have always had proper appreciation of the friendly Soviet aid which began under Stalin's leadership. We have always considered that the Soviet people's friendly aid has played a beneficial role in helping China to lay the preliminary foundations for her socialist industrialization. For this the Chinese Communist Party and the Chinese people have expressed their gratitude on numerous occasions.

In recent years the leaders of the CPSU have habitually played the benefactor and frequently boasted of their "disinterested assistance." When commemorating the 14th anniversary of the signing of the Sino-Soviet

From *Peking Review*, no. 19, 1964.

Treaty of Friendship, Alliance and Mutual Assistance in February this year, *Pravda, Izvestiia,* and other Soviet propaganda media again beat the drum to the same tune. We have not yet made a systematic reply in the press, but we must point out that, so far from being gratis, Soviet aid to China was rendered mainly in the form of trade and that it was certainly not a one-way affair. China has paid and is paying the Soviet Union in goods, gold or convertible foreign exchange for all Soviet-supplied complete sets of equipment and other goods, including those made available on credit plus interest. It is necessary to add that the prices of many of the goods we imported from the Soviet Union were much higher than those on the world market. . . .

As for the Soviet loans to China, it must be pointed out that China used them mostly for the purchase of war material from the Soviet Union, the greater part of which was used up in the war to resist U.S. aggression and aid Korea. In the war against U.S. aggression the Korean people carried by far the heaviest burden and sustained by far the greatest losses. The Chinese people, too, made great sacrifices and incurred vast military expenses. The Chinese Communist Party has always considered that this was the Chinese people's bounden internationalist duty and that it is nothing to boast of. For many years we have been paying the principal and interest on these Soviet loans, which account for a considerable part of our yearly exports to the Soviet Union. Thus even the war material supplied to China in the war to resist U.S. aggression and aid Korea has not been given gratis.

The Soviet experts working in China were invariably made welcome, respected and trusted by the Chinese government and people. The overwhelming majority of them were hard-working and helpful to China's socialist construction. We have always highly appreciated their conscientious work, and still miss them to this day.

You will remember that when the leaders of the CPSU unilaterally decided to recall all the Soviet experts in China, we solemnly affirmed our desire to have them continue their work in China and expressed the hope that the leaders of the CPSU would reconsider and change their decision.

But in spite of our objections you turned your backs on the principles guiding international relations and unscrupulously withdrew the 1,390 Soviet experts working in China, tore up 343 contracts and supplementary contracts concerning experts, and scrapped 257 projects of scientific and technical cooperation, all within the short span of a month.

You were well aware that the Soviet experts were posted in over 250 enterprises and establishments in the economic field and the fields of national defense, culture, education, and scientfic research, and that they were undertaking important tasks involving technical design, the construction of projects, the installation of equipment, trial production, and scientific research. As a result of your peremptory orders to the Soviet experts to discontinue their work and return to the Soviet Union, many of our country's important designing and scientific research projects had to stop halfway, some of the construction projects in progress had to be suspended, and some of the factories and mines which were conducting trial production could not go into production according to schedule. Your perfidious action disrupted China's original national economic plan and inflicted enormous losses upon China's socialist construction. . . .

We would like to say in passing that, basing ourselves on the international principle of mutual assistance among countries in the socialist camp, we are very much concerned about the present economic situation in the Soviet Union. If you should feel the need for the help of Chinese experts in certain fields, we would be glad to send them.

Nobody is in a better position than you to know the real cause for the curtailment of Sino-Soviet trade over the last few years. This curtailment was precisely the result of your extending the differences from the field of ideology to that of state relations.

Your sudden withdrawal of all the Soviet experts working in China upset the schedules of construction and the production arrangements of many of our factories, mines, and other enterprises and establishments, and had a direct impact on our need for the import of complete sets of equipment. Such being the case, did you expect us to keep on buying them just for display?

Moreover, in pursuance of your policy of further imposing restrictions on and discriminating against China in the economic and commercial fields, since 1960 you have deliberately placed obstacles in the way of economic and trade negotiations between our two countries and held up or refused supplies of important goods which China needs. You have insisted on providing large amounts of goods which we do not really need or which we do not need at all, while holding back or supplying very few of the goods which we need badly. For several years you have used the trade between our two countries as an instrument for bringing political pressure to bear on China. How could this avoid cutting down the volume of Sino-Soviet trade?

From 1959 to 1961, our country suffered extraordinary natural disasters for three years in succession and could not supply you with as large quantities of agricultural produce and processed products as before. This was the result of factors beyond human control. It is utterly unreasonable for you to attack China on this account and blame her for this reduction in trade. . . .

You constantly accuse us of "going it alone" and claim that you stand for extensive economic ties and division of labor among the socialist countries. But what is your actual record in this respect?

You infringe the independence and sovereignty of fraternal countries and oppose their efforts to develop their economy on an independent basis in accordance with their own needs and potentialities.

You bully those fraternal countries whose economies are less advanced and oppose their policy of industrialization and try to force them to remain agricultural countries forever and serve as your sources of raw materials and as outlets for your goods.

You bully fraternal countries which are industrially more developed and insist that they stop manufacturing their traditional products and become accessory factories serving your industries.

Moreover, you have introduced the jungle law of the capitalist world into relations between socialist countries. You openly follow the example of the Common Market which was organized by monopoly capitalist groups. . . .

Despite the fact that the differences have grown to their present serious proportions, the Chinese Communist Party is willing to do its best for the restoration and strengthening of unity. In your letter of November 29 you merely cry for a halt to the public polemics without putting forward any concrete measures for solving the problem. We now propose to you the following concrete measures for the solution of the problem, and we hope you will consider them and give us an answer.

1. For the cessation of the public polemics it is necessary for the Chinese and Soviet parties and other fraternal parties concerned to hold various bilateral and multilateral talks in order to find through consultation a fair and reasonable formula acceptable to all and to conclude a common agreement.

2. The Chinese Communist Party consistently advocates and actively supports the convening of a meeting of representatives of all communist and workers' parties. Prior to the meeting adequate preparations should be made, and difficulties and obstacles should be overcome. Together with the other fraternal parties, we will do everything possible to insure that this meeting will be a meeting of unity on the basis of the revolutionary principles of Marxism-Leninism.

3. The resumption of talks between the Chinese and Soviet parties is a necessary preparatory step for making the meeting of the fraternal parties a success. We propose that the talks between the Chinese and Soviet parties be resumed in Peking, from October 10-25, 1964.

4. In order to make further preparations for the meeting of representa-

tives of all fraternal parties, we propose that the Sino-Soviet talks be followed by a meeting of representatives of 17 fraternal parties, namely, the parties of Albania, Bulgaria, China, Cuba, Czechoslovakia, the German Democratic Republic, Hungary, Korea, Mongolia, Poland, Rumania, the Soviet Union, and Vietnam, and the parties of Indonesia, Japan, Italy, and France.

Unite under the banner of Marxism-Leninism!

The Central Committee
of the Communist Party of China

DOCUMENT 34

*Letter from the Central Committee of the
Communist Party of the Soviet Union to the
Central Committee of the Communist
Party of China, March 7, 1964.*

DEAR COMRADES,

The Central Committee of the CPSU has received your letter of February 27, 1964. We have studied it carefully. We must tell you frankly that your letter has greatly astonished us. In this letter you again lavishly employ such words as "divisive," "factional" and "sectarian," with the help of which you attempt to accuse our Party of some sort of behind-the-scenes activity against the CPC. . . .

We could refute point by point the slanderous accusations against the CPSU made off-handedly in the February 27 letter of the Central Committee of the CPC, but we do not consider it necessary to do so now. What is the use of arguments, when you have no intention of seriously entering into the essence of the questions but instead simply pour yet another bucket of dirt over our Party? . . .

We note that after many months of stalling and delay the Central Committee of the CPC has agreed with our view concerning the necessity of continuing the bilateral meeting of representatives of the CPSU and the CPC, and afterward of preparing and calling a meeting of all the communist and workers' parties. . . .

Your proposal that the meeting of representatives of the CPC and the

From *Peking Review,* no. 19, 1964.

CPSU be held as late as October 1964 means in fact that the meeting of fraternal parties would be delayed by at least a year and that the settlement of the existing differences would thus be further postponed and these differences would be further exacerbated. In our opinion, this would only bring harm to the fraternal parties and the whole world communist movement.

We also fail to understand the motives by which you were guided in making the proposal that a preparatory meeting be called composed of representatives of only 17 fraternal parties (Albania, Bulgaria, Hungary, Vietnam, G.D.R., China, Korea, Cuba, Mongolia, Poland, Rumania, U.S.S.R., Czechoslovakia, Indonesia, Japan, Italy, and France).

We consider it appropriate to hold the preparatory meeting with the participation of representatives of all the fraternal parties that were on the drafting committee of the Moscow meeting of 1960 and that jointly prepared the Statement (Albania, Bulgaria, Hungary, Vietnam, G.D.R., China, Korea, Cuba, Mongolia, Poland, Rumania, U.S.S.R., Czechoslovakia, France, Italy, German Federal Republic, Great Britain, Finland, Argentina, Brazil, Syria, India, Indonesia, U.S.A., Japan, and Australia).

This composition, covering the main areas of the revolutionary movement, was approved at that time by all the fraternal parties, and experience showed it to be helpful to the successful conduct of the 1960 meeting and the formulation of its documents. Naturally our Party, which is charged with the duty of calling the international conference, will approach all the parties and consult with them.

Guided by all these considerations, the Central Committee of the CPSU proposes:

1. That the meeting of representatives of the CPSU and the CPC be continued in Peking in May 1964.

2. That the preparatory meeting of representatives of 26 fraternal parties be called in June-July 1964.

3. That the international meeting be held with the agreement of the fraternal parties, in the autumn of 1964.

The Central Committee of the CPSU emphasizes that for the successful implementation of all these measures it is necessary that there be a cessation of public polemics and an abandonment of all types of subversive and schismatic activity in the socialist community and the communist movement.

We hope that the Central Committee of the CPC will agree to these proposals and will make its constructive contribution to the preparation and implementation of the projected measures. Our proposal of these measures is prompted by deep concern for the settlement of the differences and for the unity of the international communist movement, and these measures are in accord with the fundamental interests of the peoples of the socialist countries, the working class and the working people of all countries, and with the interests of communism.

With comradely greetings,

The Central Committee
of the Communist Party of the Soviet Union

DOCUMENT 35

Letter from the Central Committee of the Communist Party of China to the Central Committee of the Communist Party of the Soviet Union, May 7, 1964.

DEAR COMRADES!

The Central Committee of the Communist Party of China has received the letter of the Central Committee of the Communist Party of the Soviet Union dated March 7, 1964.

In your letter you tirelessly talk of the fact that it is necessary "to settle existing differences as soon as possible," "to halt open polemics among Communist Parties" and "to make every effort" to "assist the strengthening of the unity of the Communist movement." However, as the facts show, all these beautiful phrases of yours are calculated entirely for deceiving people. Neither before nor after this letter of yours have you ceased your attacks on the Communist Party of China and other fraternal Marxist-Leninist parties. At every conference, without exception, that has been held by international democratic organizations in recent months, you have propagated and forced through your erroneous line and have engaged in anti-Chinese activity. . . .

As for a meeting of CPCP and CPSU representatives and a conference of representatives of the fraternal parties of the entire world, we proposed in our letter of February 29, 1964, that meetings between CPC and CPSU representatives resume in October of this year for the purpose of preparing for a conference of representatives of fraternal parties of the entire world; that subsequently there should be a meeting of representatives of 17 frater-

From *Peking Review,* no. 19, 1964.

nal parties for the purpose of further preparation for a conference of representatives of the fraternal parties of the entire world; that after successful completion of preparatory work, the conference of representatives of fraternal parties of the entire world should be convened so that it would be an assembly of solidarity on the basis of the revolutionary principles of Marxism-Leninism.

However, in your March 7, 1964, letter you did not agree to this rational proposal and accused us of deliberate delay. You proposed holding the meeting of CPC and CPSU representatives in May, a preparatory meeting of representatives of fraternal parties in June-July, and an international conference of fraternal parties of the entire world in the autumn of this year.

What enthusiasm and activeness on your part, at first glance! However, in proposing such a tight schedule, you are by no means striving to overcome differences and strengthen solidarity. On the contrary, more and more facts provide evidence that you are planning by this step to accelerate an open split in the international Communist movement.

As early as February 12, 1964, behind our backs, you circulated among fraternal parties a letter directed against the Communist Party of China. In your February 22, 1964, letter you gave us to understand that in the anti-Chinese letter in question you had called upon them to "rebuff" us, to "take collective measures." But on February 14 and 15 you had already decided, at the CPSU Central Committee plenary session, to "come out openly and resolutely against the incorrect views and dangerous actions of the CPC leadership." This means that you have loaded the rifle and are prepared to shoot. Does not your proposal to hold a meeting of CPC and CPSU representatives in May of this year "to settle existing differences as soon as possible" look thoroughly hypocritical in the light of all this?

To judge by the present state of affairs, a meeting of CPC and CPSU representatives is not only impossible in May but would even be premature in October of this year. We think that it would be more desirable to shift the meeting of the CPC and CPSU representatives to the first half of next year—say, the month of May. If at that time either side, the CPC or the CPSU, thinks that the time for such a meeting is still not ripe, it might be postponed again. . . .

At present there is no international organization like the Third International, there is no permanent agency that would have the right to call an international conference, as was done under the Third International. In these conditions, it should not happen, indeed it is impermissible, that one party or group of parties, in violation of the principle of consulting and achieving unity among fraternal parties, should make a unilateral decision to convene a conference of representatives of all Communist and Workers' Parties, since such an action would be illegitimate and completely mistaken and would entail serious consequences. Both you and we and all the Communist and Workers' Parties know this. If the CPSU Central Committee acts autocratically and, disregarding our advice and the advice of many fraternal parties, nevertheless gathers the representatives of the segment of the parties that supports your erroneous revisionist and schismatic line, hastily holds a sort of conference and presents it as a conference of representatives of all the Communist and Workers' Parties of the world, then you will be censured for all to hear by the working class, the revolutionary peoples of the entire world, and all genuine Marxist-Leninist parties, you will bear the responsibility for a split, and the banner of so-called solidarity that you brandish will be cast to the winds. Do you want to go this far? Do you want to get into such a blind alley? We have here sincerely and honestly told you what will bring good and what will bring harm. Do not say later on that we did not warn you. . . .

With fraternal greetings.

Central Committee
of the Communist Party of China.

DOCUMENT 36

Letter from the Central Committee of the
Communist Party of the Soviet Union
to the Central Committee of the Communist
Party of China, June 15, 1964.

DEAR COMRADES,

The Central Committee of the Communist Party of the Soviet Union has received your letter of May 7, which contains an answer to ours of March 7 last. In your letter you not only reject all the proposals of the CPSU and other Marxist-Leninist Parties aimed at overcoming the difficulties in the communist movement, but virtually refuse to meet with representatives of parties, to hold talks and discuss with them common porblems of concern to the Communists of the whole world. Never before has the CC CPC so frankly expressed its scorn of the opinion of fraternal parties, and its refusal

From *Peking Review*, no. 31, 1964.

to lend ear to them and take part in a joint search for ways of overcoming the differences. . . .

Since the CC CPC is turning the question of the composition of the Meeting into another point of difference, we consider it necessary to state our attitude to it. We are of the opinion that all those parties which took part in the Meetings of 1957 and 1960 and signed their documents are entitled to attend. This is all the more so because the differences in the communist movement concern the interpretation of the Declaration and Statement. Obviously, only a forum of the parties which formulated and signed these documents are in a position to interpret them correctly. Only the conference itself has a right to decide whether any new participants should be invited. In the years that have passed since the last world Meeting there have arisen in several countries (including some African countries) parties which agree with and implement the general line of the communist movement expressed in the Declaration and Statement and are the recognized spokesmen of the working-class movement of their countries. Naturally, those parties are entitled to expect an invitation to attend the new international meeting.

But when the CC CPC poses the question of inviting new participants to the Meeting, it is thinking not of those parties but of the anti-party factional groups which it has brought into being and which it designates by the high-sounding name of "parties." However, those groups do not represent the working-class movement of their countries but have been artificially set up from without. It is no chance coincidence that the anti-party groups in Australia, Brazil, Belgium, Ceylon, and some other countries sprang up just when the CC CPC launched its factional activities within the world communist movement. Secondly, those groups do not adhere, either in theory or in practice, to the general line of the world communist movement defined in the Declaration and Statement. On the contrary, the views they advocate betray them completely as opponents of this line. Thirdly, they are made up of anti-party opposition elements expelled from Marxist-Leninist parties and fighting against lawfully elected central committees, against tested leaders of those parties who enjoy prestige. It is indicative of the political character and composition of those groups that they have been joined by Trotskyists, anarchists and all manner of renegades and apostates. It should be said in so many words that this type of adherents to the Chinese leadership's line is no credit to it. No matter how hard you try to represent those imposters as "true revolutionaries," they are outside the communist movement, and no power on earth can drag them into its ranks. . . .

The CC CPSU should like to hope that the CC CPC studies the proposals made in this letter with all seriousness, once again weighs all the possible consequences of the stand taken by it and, on its part, takes steps that would lead to unity with all Marxist-Leninist Parties rather than to a split.

With fraternal greetings,

Central Committee
of the Communist Party of the Soviet Union

DOCUMENT 37

Letter from the Central Committee of the Communist Party of the Soviet Union to the Central Committee of the Communist Party of China, July 30, 1964.

DEAR COMRADES!

The Central Committee of the CPSU has sent to all the fraternal Parties its letter of June 15 addressed to the Central Committee of the Communist Party of China. The letter sets our positions on the basic questions connected with the existing differences in the international communist movement, and also advances concrete proposals on measures for strengthening its unity.

Up to the present, an absolute majority of the fraternal Parties have spoken out in favor of the necessity for collective action to overcome the difficulties which have sprung up in our ranks. They advocate the holding of a new international meeting of representatives of the Communist and Workers' Parties, and, moreover, many Parties insist that the convening of the meeting must not be postponed for a long time. . . .

The CC of the CPSU invites the representatives of the fraternal Parties listed above to come to Moscow by December 15, 1964, so as to start on the practical work of preparation for an international meeting.

Undoubtedly, it would conform to the common wish if the committee could start working with its full membership from the beginning. However, in our opinion, the committee should also begin its work in the case that any of the 26 Communist Parties fails to send its representatives by the appointed time.

In accordance with the experience of past meetings, the drafting committee will prepare drafts of the principal documents to be submitted to the international meeting for discussion. The committee could discuss the whole range of questions concerning the holding of the international meeting and put forward its proposals on them. The drafting committee should send its proposals and recommendations on all these questions to all the fraternal Parties. . . .

In order to enable us to keep all the fraternal Parties informed of the preparatory work for the meeting, we request you to communicate to us the composition of your delegation to take part in the work of the drafting committee.

With communist greetings,

The Central Committee
of the Communist Party of the Soviet Union

DOCUMENT 38

Letter from the Central Committee of the Communist Party of China to the Central Committee of the Communist Party of the Soviet Union, August 30, 1964.

DEAR COMRADES,

The Central Committee of the Communist Party of China has received the letter of the Central Committee of the Communist Party of the Soviet Union dated July 30, 1964. Completely ignoring the desire of many fraternal Parties for unity and their opposition to a split, your letter slams the door tight against consultations on the question of convening an international meeting of the fraternal Parties and issues the order for an open split in the international communist movement. . . .

In your letter you arbitrarily lay it down that a drafting committee shall be convened without the prior attainment of unanimous agreement through bilateral and multilateral talks by the Chinese and Soviet Parties and all the other fraternal Parties concerned. The members of the drafting committee must be the 26 Parties you have designated, no more and no less, and there is no room for any discussion on this question. Every member Party of the drafting committee must immediately submit to you a list of its delegates who must report in Moscow before December 15 without fail.

You even decide before the convening of your appointed drafting committee that an international meeting shall be held in the middle of next year.

From *Peking Review*, no. 36, 1964.

Furthermore, you have the effrontery to declare in your letter that, whether or not the fraternal Parties participate, the drafting committee you have designated shall open shop as scheduled and the international meeting unilaterally called by you shall begin on the date prescribed.

Thus the day in December 1964 on which you convene your drafting committee will go down in history as the day of the great split in the international communist movement. . . .

We will never be taken in by your fine words, never submit to your threats, never be accomplices in your divisive activities, and never share with you the responsibility for splitting the international communist movement. If we were to take part in your schismatic meeting, it would be tantamount to legalizing your illegal activities, to recognizing your right to destroy the principles guiding relations among fraternal Parties as laid down in the Declaration and the Statement, and to accepting the CPSU as a patriarchal father Party. Naturally we will never act in this way, for we hold ourselves bound by principles and responsible to history. . . .

With fraternal greetings,

The Central Committee
of the Communist Party of China

By-Products and Aftermath of the Sino-Soviet Encounter

DOCUMENT 39

Letter from the Central Committee of the Communist Party of the Soviet Union to the Central Committee of the Communist Party of Japan, April 18, 1964.

DEAR COMRADES!

The Central Committee of the Communist Party of the Soviet Union has decided to send you the present letter in order to set forth once again our views on questions linked with the relations between the CPSU and the Communist Party of Japan.

The CPSU, conscious of the historical importance of the unity and solidarity of the Communists of the whole world, has undertaken and is undertaking persistent efforts aimed at overcoming the split and the difficulties in the ranks of the world Communist movement. . . .

We greeted with great satisfaction the decision of the CPJ Central Committee to send a delegation to Moscow to discuss questions of mutual interest to our parties. The CPSU Central Committee attached great significance to the meeting with the CPJ delegation, hoping that it would make it possible to reach mutual understanding and to halt the process of the deterioration of relations between our parties. . . .

Between March 2 and March 11, 1964, five long meetings of the two delegations were held. From the very beginning the CPSU delegation repeatedly offered to exchange views on fundamental problems in the international Communist movement and relations between the two parties. However, your delegation refused to discuss these questions. Hakamada, the head of the delegation, said: "We have differences on questions of princi-

From *The Current Digest of the Soviet Press* (published weekly at Columbia University), Vol. XVI, No. 32, pp. 11-13, 16. © 1964 by The Joint Committee on Slavic Studies and reprinted by permission of *The Current Digest of the Soviet Press*. Originally in *Partiinaia Zhizn*, no. 14, 1964, pp. 8-9.

ple" but "we do not intend to engage in a full, thorough and all-round exchange of views on these questions."

Instead of a frank discussion of questions of principle, the CPJ delegation devoted all its efforts to accusing the CPSU, contrary to the facts, of "interfering in the affairs of the CPJ." As the members of the CPJ Central Committe can read in the stenographic transcript, Comrade Hakamada and other comrades in the delegation advanced a number of "claims" against the CPSU. The real meaning of these efforts can be seen in the fact that the CPJ delegation advanced these claims in the form of ultimatums, with the threat that it would sever relations. Comrade Hakamada declared in his very first speech that "there is a danger of a rupture in relations." At the final meeting Comrade Hakamada said that "there is no longer even a semblance of unity between us." The CPJ delegation categorically refused to sign any kind of joint communiqué on the talks between the two parties. . . .

One of the CPJ delegation's chief complaints was that the CPSU allegedly "imposed" on your party the 1951 program and "ultraleft-wing and adventurist tactics" during the Korean War. The CPSU delegation proved the full insolvency of such fabrications on the basis of available archive documents. Our delegation showed that the CPSU had nothing to do with the "ultraleft-wing, adventurist"—as Comrade Hakamada characterized them—tactics of the CPJ during the Korean War. These tactics were in large measure a dogmatic aping of the experience of the Communist Party of China (preparations for carrying out guerrilla warfare in mountainous regions, the setting up of "support bases," etc.), and in fact they disturbed the leadership of the CPSU. . . .

With communist greetings.

Central Committee
of the Communist Party of the Soviet Union.

DOCUMENT 40

Letter from the Central Committee of the
Communist Party of Japan to the Central
Committee of the Communist Party of
the Soviet Union, July 15, 1964.

COMRADES:

Your July 11 letter was received on July 14. We regret very much that in that letter you made a series of fresh, groundless charges against our Party. . . .

Your allegation that our Party delegation "avoided a frank talk, refused to discuss questions of joint struggle against our common enemy" can only be construed as a deliberate slander against our Party in completely distorting the facts.

You also charged that our Party delegation refused to sign a joint communiqué. But, the reason why it did not agree to draft a joint communiqué was, as had already been told you in Moscow, that, if the contents of the talks were to be made public as they actually took place it would have exposed our differences before the enemy, while to make public what was contrary to the contents of the talks would be tantamount to deceiving the members of our Party and the Japanese laboring people. Furthermore, you attempted to impose on us a draft joint communiqué which had nothing to do with what actually happened at the talks; that was why our Party delegation did not agree to the issuing of any joint communiqué. You have no justification at all to blame our Party for not agreeing to issue any joint communiqué with your Party. . . .

At the very time when our Party delegation was having talks in Moscow, you carried out activities behind our backs and strengthened your contacts with Yoshio Shiga and others which had started earlier, aiding and abetting them in their anti-Party activities. This is now an open "secret." When Yoshio Shiga and Ichizo Suzuki declared their sabotage activities against our Party in flagrant violation of the Leninist principle of organization, Radio Moscow and *Pravda* lost no time in giving this group of renegades unqualified support. What is more, you deliberately withheld from your

---

From *Peking Review*, no. 31, 1964. A Soviet letter of July 11, 1964, to the Japanese Communists may be found in *The Current Digest of the Soviet Press*, vol. XVI, no. 32. Japanese letters of March 6, 1963, Jan. 10, 1964, to the Soviets appear in *Peking Review*, no. 31, 1964, and excerpts from a very long Japanese letter of Aug. 26, 1964, appear in *Peking Review*, no. 38, 1964.

readers and audience the resolution and decision explaining why the Central Committee of our Party had expelled them from our Party. Radio Moscow openly defamed the parliamentary group of our Party. Our Party refuted this, because as an independent and equal political party in the international communist movement, it could not refrain from doing so.

These clear facts are proof that after the two-Party talks, it was precisely you who launched the most brazen and unpardonable direct intervention against our Party. This shows that our delegation was entirely justified in attaching special importance during the Moscow talks to this question of your interference with our Party.

You said that we did not acquaint our Party members and organizations under its influence with the documents of the Soviet Government and the Communist Party of the Soviet Union on the international communist movement. But it is a well-known fact that we have extensively published your important documents including those in disagreement with our Party's position and views. On the contrary, it is you who have long ceased to let members of the CPSU and the Soviet people know about the important resolutions and documents of our Party. Isn't this a fact? What you want is, in the final analysis, that we should unilaterally publish your documents and unconditionally submit to your position and views. However, you have no right to demand this of our Party. As an independent political party adhering to the principles of Marxism-Leninism, our Party resolutely rejects your unreasonable and unprincipled demand. . . .

Our Party has abided by the principles of Marxism-Leninism, proletarian internationalism, the revolutionary principles of the Moscow Declaration and Statement, and the principles governing relations among farternal Parties unanimously adopted at the Moscow meeting; it will continue to work unremittingly to oppose a split in the international communist movement and to realize genuine unity. At the same time, we will resolutely reject any unjustifiable interference with our Party, no matter from which Party it may come.

With communist greetings,

The Central Committee
of the Communist Party of Japan

DOCUMENT 41

*"Statement on the Stand of the Rumanian
Workers' Party concerning the Problems of
the World Communist and Working
Class Movement," April 22, 1964 (Part II).*

OF LATE, THE divergencies in the international communist and working-class movement have deepened, and the public polemic has assumed particular sharpness. Instead of a debate imbued with the endeavor to bring standpoints closer to each other and to find solutions based on Marxist-Leninist ideology, forms and methods have been adopted in the course of the public polemic which considerably envenom relations between parties, and offensive judgments, as well as accusations and the ascribing of certain intentions are being resorted to.

Particularly serious is the fact that almost all fraternal parties are drawn into the polemic, and that the key is set by parties that owing to their merits and revolutionary experience have a great influence in the communist movement. . . .

The long history of the communist movement shows us the kind of negative results to which non-observance of the correct norms of relations between parties leads, norms based on the collective working out of decisions, on each party's independence and equal rights, on non-interference in the internal affairs of other parties. . . .

There does not and cannot exist a "parent" party and a "son-party", parties that are "superior" and parties that are "subordinate", but there exists the great family of communist and workers' parties, which have equal rights. No party has or can have a privileged place, or can impose its line and opinions on other parties. Each party makes its own contribution to the development of the common treasure store of Marxist-Leninist teaching, to enriching the forms and practical methods of revolutionary struggle for winning power and building the socialist society.

In discussing and confronting different points of view on problems concerning the revolutionary struggle or socialist construction, no party must label as anti-Marxist, anti-Leninist the fraternal party whose opinions it does not share.

We consider as unjust the practice of using in Party documents, in the

From Agerpres (Rumanian News Agency): *Documents, Articles and Information on Rumania—Supplement*, April, 1964. A portion of this resolution dealing with Comecon appears above, pp. 127-29, as "Part I".

press and over the radio, at meetings of international organizations, and so on, offensive assessments, accusations and epithets against fraternal parties and their leadership, of expounding in an unfriendly and distorted manner within the ranks of the Party or among the mass of the people the stand of other parties, of condemning at congresses or in the resolutions of a Party the point of view of other communist parties, and the stand taken by them.

No Party is allowed to bypass the Party leadership in one country or another, and so much the less, to launch appeals for the removal, or the change of the leadership of a party. Appraisals and manifestations which lack respect for a communist party and its leadership, may justly be interpreted as a lack of respect for the working class, for the people who trust the party and the leadership of the communist party of their country; and this further worsens the relations between parties, between socialist states, and affects the friendship of the respective peoples. . . .

The Communist Party of the Soviet Union and the Communist Party of China have, owing to their prestige, a particular responsibility and role in reestablishing the unity of the communist movement. We address an appeal to all the fraternal parties and above all to the two big parties, the Communist Party of the Soviet Union and the Communist Party of China: let all of us unite to bar the road to a split, to safeguard the unity and cohesion of the countries of the socialist camp, of the world communist and working-class movement!

The Central Committee
of the Rumanian Workers' Party

DOCUMENT 42

Memorandum from Togliatti to the Central Committee of the Communist Party of the Soviet Union, August 21, 1964.

THE LETTER FROM the Soviet Communist Party with the invitation to the preparatory meeting for the international conference reached Rome a few days before my departure [for a visit to Russia, during which he unexpect-

---

From *Pravda,* September 10, 1964. Editor's translation from the Russian (original in Italian). Although Togliatti did not present this as the official opinion of the Central Committee of the Italian Communist Party, his authority as general secretary of the party gives the document great weight. He died later on the day this was composed.

edly died—Ed.]. For this reason and also in view of the absence of many comrades, we have not had the possibility of considering it collectively in the party leadership. Nevertheless, it remains firmly established that we shall take part and take part actively in the preparatory meeting.

However, we retain our doubts and reservations about the opportuneness of the international conference, above all because it is now clear that, apart from the Chinese party, a group of parties that cannot be ignored will not participate. The plan we had proposed for an effective struggle against the erroneous political line and against the splitting activity of the Chinese Communists was different from the one actually followed. Fundamentally our plan was based on these points:

> Never to interrupt the polemic against the positions of principle and the political views of the Chinese.

> To conduct the polemic, contrary to Chinese practice, without verbal exacerbations and without condemnations of a general character, on concrete themes, in an objective and persuasive manner and always with a certain respect for the adversary.

> At the same time to organize groups of parties in a series of meetings for a profound examination and a better definition of the tasks presenting themselves today in different sectors of our movement. . . .

A different line was pursued, and I do not consider the results very good. Some (possibly even many) parties were expecting a conference to be convened within a short period in order to pronounce an unambiguous and solemn condemnation, binding on the whole movement. Such an expectation may even have disoriented them. In the meantime the Chinese attack has been widely developed and thus they have acted to establish small splinter groups and to attract some parties to their viewpoint. One has customarily replied to their general attack through an ideological and propagandistic polemic, not through the development of our policy in connection to the struggle against the Chinese views. . . .

Recent events in Vietnam, events in Cyprus, demonstrate in what form we may unexpectedly encounter very sharp crises and danger, especially if the trend to the right continues in international relations, and then the whole Communist movement, all of the workers' and socialists' forces in Europe and of the whole world must be deployed in all their strength. We consider it necessary to take this situation into account in all our conduct towards the Chinese Communists. The unity of all socialist forces in common action, even transcending ideological differences, against the most reactionary imperialist groups is an indispensable necessity. One cannot imagine that China or the Chinese Communists could be excluded from this unity. Consequently, from now on we must behave in such a manner as not to create obstacles on the way to achieving this objective.

In connection with the meeting of the preparatory committee on December 15 one could be thinking already about some initiatives. For example, the sending of a delegation, composed of representatives from several parties to expound to the Chinese comrades our intention of being united and of collaborating in the struggle against the common enemy, to present to them the problem of finding a way and a concrete form for this collaboration. . . .

Although we have always regarded the Chinese views as erroneous and ruinous, we have always expressed and now maintain strong reservations on the utility of an international conference dedicated solely or mainly to denunciations and to struggle against these views. For this very reason we feared and now fear that in this manner the Communist parties of the capitalist countries would be pushed into the direction opposite to the necessary one. They may envelope themselves in internal polemics of a purely ideological nature, far removed from reality. The danger would become particularly serious if one were to arrive at an open schism of the movement, with the formation of an international Chinese center which would create its "sections" in all countries. All the parties, and especially the weakest, would be placed in the position of devoting a large part of their activity to the polemic and to the battle against these so-called "sections" of a new "international."

. . . I suggest that without risk of error I may state that the unbridled and shameless campaign that the Albanians and Chinese have conducted against the CPSU, against the leadership, and especially against Comrade Khrushchev have not made any impact on the broad masses, despite the fact that it was utilized to the full by the propagandists and governments of the bourgeois countries. The authority and prestige of the Soviet Union among the broad masses remains tremendous. Even the crudest slander of the Chinese (on the Soviet Union's becoming bourgeois, etc.) has not made any mark on them. The only thing that has caused some perplexity is the question of the recall of the Soviet technical specialists from China.

But what causes unrest among the masses and also (at least in our country) a sufficiently significant proportion of the Communists is the very fact of an acute clash between two countries that both have become socialist through the victory of two great revolutions. The fact calls into question the very principles of socialism, and we must make a great effort to explain what are the historical and political conditions of the parties and personalities that have contributed to the creation of the present differences and conflicts. . . .

One fact that worries us and one we are unable to explain fully is the manifestation among the socialist countries of a centrifugal tendency. In this is concealed an undoubted and serious danger, with which, in our opinion, the Soviet comrades should concern themselves. Without doubt there is in this tendency a revival of nationalism. However, we know that national sentiment remains a permanent factor in the working class and socialist movement for a long time, even after the conquest of power. Economic progress does not dispel this, it nurtures it. Also in the socialist camp it is possible (I underline the world possible because many concrete facts are unknown to us) that one must caution oneself against forced, exterior uniformity and one must consider that unity ought to be established and maintained in conditions of diversity and full autonomy of the individual countries. . . .

DOCUMENT 43

Communiqué of the Consultative Meeting of Representatives of Communist and Workers' Parties, Moscow, March 10, 1965.

A CONSULTATIVE MEETING was held in Moscow March 1-5 of representatives of the Communist Party of Australia, the Communist Party of Argentina, the Bulgarian Communist Party, the Brazilian Communist Party, the Communist Party of Great Britain, the Hungarian Socialist Workers' Party, the Socialist Unity Party of Germany, the Communist Party of Germany, the Communist Party of India, the Italian Communist Party, the United Party of the Socialist Revolution of Cuba, the Mongolian People's Revolutionary Party, the Polish United Workers' Party, the Syrian Communist Party, the Communist Party of the Soviet Union, the Communist Party of Finland, the French Communist Party, and the Communist Party of Czechoslovakia. Representatives of the Communist Party of the United States of America attended the meeting as observers.

From *The Current Digest of the Soviet Press* (published weekly at Columbia University), Vol. XVII, No. 9, pp. 7-8. © 1965 by *The Joint Committee on Slavic Studies* and reprinted by permission of *The Current Digest of the Soviet Press*. Originally in *Pravda*, March 10, 1965, p. 1.

The participants in the meeting held consultations on questions of mutual interest and exchanged opinions on ways for overcoming disagreements and strengthening the solidarity of the world Communist movement.

The meeting proceeded in an atmosphere of fraternity and friendship and was permeated with a spirit of active struggle for the solidarity of the Communist movement for the sake of fulfilling its great historical tasks. The participants in the meeting expressed the firm determination of their parties to do everything in their power to consolidate the international Communist movement, to strengthen its unity on the basis of Marxism-Leninism and proletarian internationalism, on the basis of the line defined by the 1957 Declaration and the 1960 Statement. . . .

The participants in the meeting held unanimously that in today's conditions, as the 1960 Statement points out, international conferences of Communist and Workers' Parties are an effective form for the mutual exchange of opinions and experience, for enriching Marxist-Leninist theory through collective efforts and working out single positions in the struggle for common goals. Such conferences, carried out with the observance of the principles of full equality and the independence of each party, can well serve the cause of overcoming disagreements and consolidating the Communist movement on the basis of Marxism-Leninism and proletarian internationalism. Therefore the active and thorough preparation of a new international conference and its convocation at a suitable time, in the opinion of the participants in the meeting, fully answer the interests of the world Communist movement [no such conference had been convened by the end of 1966— ED.].

The War in Vietnam
and the Sino-Soviet Stalemate

DOCUMENT 44

*"Refutation of the New Leaders of the
Communist Party of the Soviet Union on
'United Action,'" November 10, 1965*

. . . The new leaders of the CPSU never weary of saying that, however serious the differences between them, communists must take "united action" on the question of Vietnam at this urgent juncture in the Vietnamese people's struggle against the United States.

Since the new leaders of the CPSU have destroyed the basis of international proletarian unity, and since they transpose enemies and friends and persist in the line of Soviet-U.S. collaboration for world domination, is it still possible for the Marxist-Leninist parties to take united action with them on the question of Vietnam?

At a time when the U.S. imperialists are committing rabid aggression against Vietnam, all communist parties and socialist countries should as a matter of course take a unanimous stand and firmly support the Vietnamese people's just struggle to smash this aggression. The point is that the stand taken by the revisionist leadership of the CPSU on the question of Vietnam is inseparable from their revisionist program and line, and is contrary to the principled stand required of a Marxist-Leninist party.

When Khrushchev was in power, the revisionist leadership of the CPSU openly sided with U.S. imperialism and opposed and undermined the revolutionary struggle of the Vietnamese people against U.S. aggression. They alleged that "any small 'local war' might spark off the conflagration of a world war." Using this absurd argument to frighten and intimidate all peoples engaged in revolutionary armed struggle, they openly refused to support and aid the Vietnamese people in their anti-U.S. struggle. When the struggles of the Vietnamese and the Laotian peoples against U.S. imperial-

From *Peking Review*, no. 46, 1965. The authorship of the article is given as "The editorial departments of *Jen-min Jih-pao* and *Hung-chi*."

ism grew acute, their policy on the question of Indo-China was one of "disengagement." . . .

The situation in Vietnam developed directly contrary to the wishes of the Khrushchev revisionists. The Vietnamese people won victory after victory in their revolutionary anti-U.S. struggle, while the U.S. aggressors grew hard pressed. The new leaders of the CPSU came to realize that it was no longer advisable to copy Khrushchev's policy of "disengagement" in its totality. So they switched to the policy of involvement, that is, of getting their hand in.

The policy of involvement and the policy of disengagement are essentially the same. Both are products of Khrushchev revisionism and both are designed to meet the needs of U.S. imperialism. . . .

The new leaders of the CPSU are doing exactly what Khrushchev did before them, namely, pulling the Vietnam question into the orbit of Soviet-U.S. collaboration. Since they are cooperating so closely with the U.S. imperialists in united action, it is of course impossible for Marxist-Leninists to join in and take "united action" with them.

At bottom, the new leaders of the CPSU are clamoring for "united action" on the Vietnam question because this slogan is highly deceptive and is apt to create the illusion that it is still possible to have "unity against U.S. imperialism" with the new leaders of the CPSU who are intent on Soviet-U.S. collaboration for world domination. They do so in order to worm their way into the anti-U.S. front and carry out their policy of involvement in the service of U.S. imperialism. . . .

Furthermore, the new leaders of the CPSU have been using their "aid" to Vietnam as a pretext for wantonly vilifying China, and have been assiduously spreading the lie that "China obstructed the transit of Soviet military equipment for Vietnam." The truth is that we have always honored our agreements and done our utmost speedily to transport to Vietnam all military material in transit which was furnished by the Soviet Union with the concurrence of the Vietnamese comrades. By these fabrications and slanders, the new leaders of the CPSU have supplied further proof that they stop at nothing in order to ally themselves with the United States against China. . . .

Things could not be clearer. If we were to take united action on the question of Vietnam with the new leaders of the CPSU who are pursuing the Khrushchev revisionist line, wouldn't we be helping them to deceive the people of the world? Wouldn't we be helping them to bring the question of Vietnam within the orbit of Soviet-U.S. collaboration? Wouldn't we be joining them in betraying the revolutionary cause of the Vietnamese people? Wouldn't we be joining them in attacking the Chinese Communist Party and all the other Marxist-Leninist parties? Wouldn't we be joining them in serving as accomplices of U.S. imperialism? Of course, we shall do nothing of the sort. . . .

DOCUMENT 45

Letter from the Central Committee of the Communist Party of the Soviet Union to other Communist Parties, probably March, 1966.

THE CENTRAL COMMITTEE of the Communist Party of the Soviet Union deems it necessary to inform you of our position on the new steps taken by the Chinese Communist Party that are aimed at strengthening the divisive line in the socialist community [commonwealth?—ED.] and in the Communist world movement, as well as of the conclusion we draw from these facts.

We deem it all the more expedient as the CPSU engages in no open polemics against the fabrications of the Chinese leaders, does not answer their attacks in the press, but merely states its views in a positive way. . . .

As you know, the CCP leadership in an article published on November 11, 1965 [see Document 44; the U.S. Consulate General, Hong Kong, gives the date as November 10—ED.] in *Jen-min Jih-pao* and in *Hung-chi* demonstratively rejected joint action with other socialist countries in the struggle against imperialism and primarily for the protection of fraternal Vietnam against predatory United States aggression. . . .

The Soviet Union delivers large amounts of weapons to the D.R.V. [Democratic Republic of Vietnam, North Vietnam—ED.] including rocket installations, anti-aircraft artillery, airplanes, tanks, coastal artillery, warships and other items. In 1965 alone weapons and other war material worth about 500 million rubles ($550 million) were placed at the disposal of the D.R.V. The D.R.V. is receiving support in the training of pilots, rocket personnel, tank drivers, artillerymen, and so on. Our military aid is being rendered to the extent the Vietnamese leadership itself thinks necessary.

From *Die Welt,* Hamburg, March 21, 1966; and *The New York Times,* March 24, 1966. Reprinted by permission. This letter was not published by any Communist source, but was somehow leaked to *Die Welt,* Hamburg. The existence of a letter along these lines was established by the letter of the Chinese Communist Party to the Soviet party, dated March 22, 1966, in which the Chinese declined to send a delegation to the twenty-third congress of the CPSU (*Peking Review,* March 25, 1966).

The Soviet Union grants extensive military and material support to the National Liberation Front of South Vietnam.

The CPSU has proposed to the Chinese leaders more than once that joint action to support Vietnam be organized. But the Chinese leaders opposed such action by the socialist states. In connection with the expansion of the United States aggression against the D.R.V. our party has proposed twice that the representatives of the three parties—the Vietnamese Workers' Party, the CPSU and the CCP—meet at the highest level to achieve agreement on coordinated action for the aid of the D.R.V. These proposals, which were received by the Central Committee of the Workers' Party of Vietnam with approval were not accepted by the Chinese leaders.

At the same time, the CCP leadership hindered the implementation of the agreement of the government of the U.S.S.R. with the government of the D.R.V. on an immediate increase in military aid for the D.R.V. The CCP leaders did not permit Soviet transport planes with weapons to fly over CCP territory.

Then Chinese personalities also place obstacles in the way of the transportation of war materiel to Vietnam by rail. Thus at their [the Vietnamese —ED.] request, an additional shipment of military equipment, including anti-aircraft artillery, which is needed urgently to protect the Vietnamese cities and villages against the United States pirates, was recently delivered to the Vietnamese comrades. The Chinese authorities refused for a long time to relay the freight under the pretense that papers for its transit had not yet been filled out and they did not know "whether Vietnam needs this war materiel." . . .

From all this it becomes clear that the Chinese leaders need a lengthy Vietnam war to maintain international tensions, to represent China as "a besieged fortress." There is every reason to assert that it is one of the goals of the Chinese leadership to originate a military conflict between the U.S.S.R. and the United States. They want a clash of the U.S.S.R. and the United States so that they may, as they themselves say, "sit on the mountain and watch the fight of the tigers." . . .

[Presumably signed by the Central Committee, CPSU]

Conclusion

BOTH COMMUNISTS and non-Communists have had difficulty in finding a suitable name for the conglomeration of Communist parties and states that has existed since the dissolution of the Comintern. "Movement," "camp," and "commonwealth" (the latter two terms referring only to Communist-ruled countries, not parties out of power) are the principal Communist attempts at labeling. "Empire," "bloc," and "system" (the former two referring, again, only to Communist countries) have been proposed by non-Communist analysts. But such terms all turn out to be inaccurate or excessively vague ("camp," "empire," and "bloc" have been increasingly inapplicable since Tito's rift with Stalin in 1948; "movement," "commonwealth," and "system" do not convey much in particular). In fact, all efforts at finding a familiar name—or model—corresponding to the reality of Communism around the world are probably doomed by the historical uniqueness and changing makeup of this reality. What the world has had since 1943 is a number of national Communist parties and states whose interrelations have been diverse, complex, and in some cases unstable. It is probably more revealing to perceive this question as a special branch of international relations than to start with the Marxian myth of proletarian unity and its implication that there is a firm organization.

But is it worth repeating that it is a *special* kind of international relations, characterized by peculiar institutions, practices, and ideological concerns, that the preceding pages have suggested. It is also special in a way that has not been explicitly emphasized in this book: the *exclusiveness* of the Communists in their international dealings. Theirs is a closed network of alignments and antagonisms, which non-Communists cannot penetrate. Most Communist states are members of the United Nations; heads of Western states exchange visits with some Communist regimes; and even China attended the Bandung conference, in the days before relations with India and Indonesia soured. But none of these international contacts bring the non-Communists into immediate participation in the international relations among Communists. The outsiders cannot become allies or mediators in inter-Communist disputes, nor are these conflicts likely to be considered in the United Nations, with or without the admission of China.

By the same token, non-Communists have demonstrated little ability in stirring up antagonisms among Communists, much as some may desire this.

It is not surprising that the spontaneous emergence of inter-Communist conflicts, especially the Sino-Soviet quarrel, has been welcomed by many anti-Communists, but their satisfaction may be self-delusion. The threat of indefinite Communist expansion is probably not based on the total numbers of troops (or party members) that any Communist center can marshal under one command. From a military point of view, it is highly unlikely, for instance, that the capability of the Soviet nuclear-armed missile force or its conventional force is lessened by the Sino-Soviet dispute. American difficulties with a Communist guerrilla army in Vietnam during a time of deep Sino-Soviet antagonism should dispel any hopes that rifts among Communists solve the security problems of non-Communists. While splits within such Communist parties out of power as those in Brazil or India may be a source of immediate Communist weakness in those countries, the emergence of an ultra-militant, Maoist breed of Communists should discourage complacency among non-Communists. Also, the increasing possibility of a sovereign national Communist party—a by-product of dissension among Communists—may make Communism more attractive to uncommitted leftists in underdeveloped countries.

In sum, the strains and antagonisms among Communist states and parties in some ways are ominous trends for the outside world, representing increasingly serious threats to peace that cannot be eased by such means of resolving conflicts as the non-Communist world has developed. At the same time, the threat to peace through Communist efforts to take power in more and more countries seems hardly reduced by the divergencies among Communists.

In time, however, the failure of Communists to work out a viable community of their own may undermine the mythology of proletarian unity on which their exclusiveness is based. Gradually, international relations among Communists may then blend into international relations as a whole, which should be a net gain for the cause of peace.

Guide
to Further Study

BIBLIOGRAPHICAL AND RELATED GUIDES

Hammond, Thomas T. (ed.), *Soviet Foreign Relations and World Communism: A Selected Annotated Bibliography of 7,000 Books in 30 Languages.* Princeton: Princeton University Press, 1965.

Kolarz, Walter (ed.), *Books on Communism, a Bibliography.* New York: Oxford University Press, 1964.

Roberts, Henry L. (ed.), *Foreign Affairs Bibliography: A Selected and Annotated List of Books on International Relations 1942-1952.* New York: Council on Foreign Relations, 1955. Same for period 1952-1962, published 1964.

Triska, Jan, and Robert M. Slusser, *A Calendar of Soviet Treaties, 1917-1957.* Stanford: Stanford University Press, 1959.

GENERAL WORKS
(1) Documents

(a) Serial publications that often contain documents on international relations among Communists

Current Digest of the Soviet Press (New York)

East Europe (New York)

New Times (Moscow)

Peking Review (Peking)

Royal Institute of International Affairs, *Documents on International Affairs* (London, annual)

United States Consulate General, Hong Kong, *Current Background* (Hong Kong)

United States Consulate General, Hong Kong, *Survey of the China Mainland Press* (Hong Kong)

World Marxist Review (London).

(b) Books

Dallin, Alexander, Jonathan Harris, and Grey Hodnett (eds.), *Diversity in International Communism: A Documentary Record, 1961-1963.* New York: Columbia University Press, 1963.

Russian Institute, Columbia University, *The Anti-Stalin Campaign and International Communism: A Selection of Documents.* New York: Columbia University Press, 1956.

(2) *Secondary Studies*

Aspaturian, Vernon V., *The Soviet Union in the World Communist System.* Stanford: The Hoover Institution, 1966.

Black, C. E. and Thomas P. Thornton (eds.), *Communist Revolution.* Princeton: Princeton University Press, 1964.

Bromke, Adam (ed.), *The Communist States at the Crossroads Between Moscow and Peking.* New York: Frederick A. Praeger, 1965.

Brzezinski, Zbigniew, *The Soviet Bloc: Unity and Conflict.* New York: Frederick A. Praeger, 1960.

Grzybowski, Kazimierz, *The Socialist Commonwealth of Nations: Organizations and Institutions.* New Haven, Yale University Press, 1964.

Gyorgy, Andrew (ed.), *Issues of World Communism.* Princeton: Van Nostrand, 1966.

Kaser, Michael, *Comecon: Integration Problems of the Planned Economies.* London: Oxford University Press, 1965.

Labedz, Leopold (ed.), *International Communism after Khrushchev.* Cambridge: M.I.T. Press, 1965.

Laqueur, Walter and Labedz, Leopold (eds.), *Polycentrism: The New Factor in International Communism.* New York: Frederick A. Praeger, 1963.

Lowenthal, Richard, *World Communism: The Distintegration of a Secular Faith.* New York: Oxford University Press, 1964.

Modelski, George, *Atomic Energy in the Communist Bloc.* Cambridge: Cambridge University Press, 1959.

Nollau, Gunther, *International Communism and World Revolution: History and Methods.* New York: Frederick A. Praeger, 1961.

Pethyridge, Roger (ed.), *The Development of the Communist Bloc.* Boston: D. C. Heath and Co., 1965.

Pryor, Frederick L., *The Communist Foreign Trade System.* Cambridge: M.I.T. Press, 1963.

Seton-Watson, Hugh, *From Lenin to Khrushchev.* New York: Frederick A. Praeger, 1951.

EUROPE (INCLUDING SOVIET UNION)
(1) *Documents*

Bass, Robert and Elizabeth Marbury (eds.), *The Soviet-Yugoslav Controversy, 1948-1958: A Documentary Record.* New York: Prospect Books, 1959.

Benes, Vaclav, Robert F. Byrnes, and Nicholas Spulber (eds.), *The Second Soviet-Yugoslav Dispute: The Full Text of the Main Documents.* Bloomington: Indiana University, Russian and East European Institute, 1959.

The Correspondence Between the Central Committee of the Communist Party of Yugoslavia and the Central Committee of the All-Union Communist Party (Bolsheviks). Belgrade: Jugoslovenska Knjiga, 1948.

Griffith, William E., *Albania and the Sino-Soviet Rift*. Cambridge: M.I.T. Press, 1963.

Royal Institute of International Affairs, *The Soviet-Yugoslav Dispute*. London: Royal Institute of International Affairs, 1948.

Yugoslavia, Ministry of Foreign Affairs, *White Book on Aggressive Activities by the Governments of the USSR, Poland, Czechoslovakia, Hungary, Rumania, Bulgaria and Albania towards Yugoslavia*. Belgrade: Ministry of Foreign Affairs of the Federal Republic of Yugoslavia, 1951.

Zinner, Paul E. (ed.), *National Communism and Popular Revolt in Eastern Europe: A Selection of Documents on Events in Poland and Hungary, February-November, 1956*. New York: Columbia University Press, 1956.

(2) Secondary Studies

Brown, J. F., *The New Eastern Europe: The Khrushchev Era and After*. New York: Frederick A. Praeger, 1966.

Dziewanowski, M. K., *The Communist Party of Poland: an Outline of History*. Cambridge: Harvard University Press, 1959.

Fischer-Galati, Stephen (ed.), *Eastern Europe in the Sixties*. New York: Frederick A. Praeger, 1963.

Floyd, David, *Rumania: Russia's Dissident Ally*. New York. Frederick A. Praeger, 1965.

Griffith, William E., *Albania and the Sino-Soviet Dispute*. Cambridge: M.I.T. Press, 1963.

————, *Communism in Europe: Continuity, Change and the Sino-Soviet Dispute*. Cambridge: M.I.T. Press, Vol. I, 1964, Vol. II, 1966.

Hoffman, George W. and Fred W. Neal, *Yugoslavia and the New Communism*. New York: The Twentieth Century Fund, 1962.

Inonescu, Ghita, *The Break-up of the Soviet Empire in Eastern Europe*. Harmondsworth: Penguin Books, 1965.

Kohler, Heinz, *Economic Integration in the Soviet Bloc with an East German Case Study*. New York: Frederick A. Praeger, 1966.

Rieber, Alfred J., *Stalin and the French Communist Party 1941-1947*. New York: Columbia University Press, 1962.

Skilling, H. Gordon, *Communism, National and International*. Toronto: University of Toronto Press, 1964.

Taborsky, Edward, *Communism in Czechoslovakia, 1948-1960*. Princeton: Princeton University Press, 1961.

Ulam, Adam, *Titoism and the Cominform*. Cambridge: Harvard University Press, 1952.

180   GUIDE TO FURTHER STUDY

Vali, Ferenec A., *Rift and Revolt in Hungary*. Cambridge: Harvard University Press, 1961.

ASIA (INCLUDING SINO-SOVIET RELATIONS)
(1) Documents

Doolin, Dennis J., *Territorial Claims in the Sino-Soviet Conflict: Documents and Analysis*. Stanford: The Hoover Institution on War, Revolution and Peace, Stanford University, 1965.

Floyd, David, *Mao against Khrushchev: A Short History of the Sino-Soviet Conflict*. New York: Frederick A. Praeger, 1963.

Griffith, William F., *The Sino-Soviet Rift*. Cambridge: M.I.T. Press, 1964.

Hudson, G. F., Richard Lowenthal, and Roderick MacFarquhar (eds.), *The Sino-Soviet Dispute*. New York: Frederick A. Praeger, 1961.

(2) Secondary Studies

Barnett, A. Doak (ed.), *Communist Strategies in Asia*. New York: Frederick A. Praeger, 1963.

Boorman, Howard L., Alexander Eckstein, Philip Moseley, and Benjamin Schwartz, *The Moscow-Peking Axis*. New York: Harper and Row, 1957.

Cheng, Chu-yuan, *Economic Relations between Peking and Moscow*. New York: Frederick A. Praeger, 1964.

Crankshaw, Edward, *The New Cold War: Moscow v. Peking*. Harmondsworth: Penguin Books, 1963.

Floyd, David, *Mao against Khrushchev: A Short History of the Sino-Soviet Conflict*. New York: Frederick A.. Praeger, 1963.

Garthoff, Raymond L. (ed.), *Sino-Soviet Military Relations*. New York: Frederick A. Praeger, 1966.

Griffith, William F., *The Sino-Soviet Rift*. Cambridge: M.I.T. Press, 1964.

Hindley, Donald, *The Communist Party of Indonesia*. Berkeley: University of California Press, 1964.

Honey, P. J., *Communism in North Viet Nam*. Cambridge, M.I.T. Press, 1963.

Kautsky, John H., *Moscow and the Communist Party of India: A Study in the Post-war Evolution of International Communist Strategy*. Cambridge: M.I.T. Press, 1956.

London, Kurt (ed.), *Unity and Contradiction: Major Aspects of Sino-Soviet Relations*. New York: Frederick A. Praeger, 1962.

Mehnert, Klaus, *Moscow and Peking*. New York: G. P. Putnam, 1963.

Scalapino, Robert A. (ed.), *The Communist Revolution in Asia: Tactics, Goals and Achievements*. Englewood Cliffs: Prentice/Hall, 1965.

Swearingen, Rodger and Paul Langer, *Red Flag in Japan. International Communism in Action 1919-1951*. Cambridge: Harvard University Press, 1952.

Zablocki, Clement J. (ed.), *The Sino-Soviet Rivalry.* New York: Frederick A. Praeger, 1966.

Zagoria, Donald S., *The Annals of the American Academy of Political and Social Science* ("Communist China and the Soviet Bloc"), Vol. 349, September, 1963.

——, *The Sino-Soviet Conflict, 1956-1961.* Princeton: Princeton University Press, 1962.

OTHER AREAS

Alexander, Robert, *Communism in Latin America.* New Brunswick: Rutgers University Press, 1957.

Brzezinski, Zbigniew (ed.), *Africa and the Communist World.* Stanford: Stanford University Press, 1963.

Morison, David L. (ed.), *The USSR and Africa.* New York: Oxford University Press, 1964.

Poppino, Rollie, *International Communism in Latin America 1917-1963.* New York: Free Press, 1964.

Other Spectrum Books of Interest